P9-CMA-244

WILD FLOWER GARDENING

WILD FLOWER GARDENING

NORMAN TAYLOR

D. VAN NOSTRAND COMPANY, INC.
PRINCETON, NEW JERSEY
TORONTO · LONDON · NEW YORK

D. VAN NOSTRAND COMPANY, INC.

120 Alexander St., Princeton, New Jersey
250 Fourth Avenue, New York 3, New York
25 Hollinger Rd., Toronto 16, Canada
Macmillan & Co., Ltd., St. Martin's St., London, W.C. 2, England

All correspondence should be addressed to the principal office of the company at Princeton, N. J.

Library of Congress Catalogue Card No. 55-9907

Published simultaneously in Canada by
D. VAN NOSTRAND COMPANY (Canada), LTD.

PRINTED IN THE UNITED STATES OF AMERICA

PREFACE

R*ECENT IMPORTANT STUDIES* of our native flora have reminded the garden public of the wealth of beautiful wild flowers that are within the range of any gardener who is willing to learn some of nature's secrets. One of these studies, a monumental book in three volumes, is the revision by Dr. H. A. Gleason of the old *Illustrated Flora* of the eastern United States, by the late N. L. Britton and Addison Brown.

That revision has been followed in this book as to the correct names of the plants here included, because it is my conviction that the garden public will turn to it for the next half century as the authority on all the plants that grow wild within our area. Of these only a handful, comparatively, can be included here—those that are most showy, most easily cultivated, and readily available. A selection of Tabea Hofmann's wild flower drawings has been reproduced with permission of the publisher from E. Wherry, *Wild Flower Guide,* Doubleday & Co., Inc.

The cultivation of wild flowers, if carried on with intelligence, is often the best method of preserving our vanishing flora. Conservation, in the face of hordes of so-called flower lovers, and of equally destructive improvements, may well become a myth. Cultivation at least provides some safeguard, as well as initiating the gardener into a realm far removed from less rewarding pursuits.

N. T.

Elmwood
Princess Anne, Maryland
March, 1955

CONTENTS

HOW TO USE THE BOOK

B*ECAUSE WOODLAND* flowers are the most numerous, and their cultivation completely depends upon the conditions in the forest, the first chapter deals only with this topic. The excuse for the chapter being so long is that it is fundamental. No one should skip it because of the desire to hurry on to the second chapter where the individual woodland plants and their culture are discussed.

Less demanding as to sites and soils are the native plants in the third chapter, devoted to plants for thickets and open places. Somewhat more specialized are the environments that seem most unfavorable, such as pure sand and the conditions at the seashore. Plants suited to these comprise Chapter IV.

So much confusion exists as to the plants suited to wet places, that Chapter V is given over to the distinction among bogs, marshes, meadows, and swamps, and the plants suited to these very different sites. In bogs also grow many orchids, but some also grow in the woods, so that Chapter VI is entirely devoted to these interesting but little-known plants.

Finally, reserved for the end, is a small group of wild plants that will baffle all but the experts or those amateurs with enough patience and skill to conquer the difficulty of growing them.

No shrubs or trees are included in the book, as most people who undertake wild gardening have enough sense and taste to fit plants into existing environments—not to create artificial "wild gardens." For quite a different reason, many beautiful wild flowers from the Pacific Coast have been excluded. Their cultivation in the East is much too precarious for the audience to whom this book is chiefly addressed.

LIST OF ILLUSTRATIONS

COLOR PLATES

The thirty-two color plates, comprising over eighty species of wild flowers are included to give the reader a small sample of the gorgeous plant material native in our country. Many of them are not usually cultivated, but those that are in the text have been cross-referenced to the appropriate plate number. Some of the Latin, and a few of the common names on the plates, due to differences in usage, do not agree with the text, but the author has indicated these in the text, so that such deviations should not confuse the reader.

THE PUBLISHERS

PLATE I

Harold D. Roberts

PASQUEFLOWER
Pulsatilla ludoviciana

Kathleen N. Marriage

LONG-SPURRED BLUE COLUMBINE
Aquilegia caerulea

Hiram L. Parent

WILD COLUMBINE
Aquilegia canadensis

PLATE 2

Walter Henricks Hodge

WHITE WATERLILY
Castalia odorata

Russell Tinling Pansie

AMERICAN LOTUS
Nelumbo pentaphylla

Woodland Garden

CHAPTER I

T*HE DESIRE* to have a wild flower garden is so natural that there is little need to advocate it. There would be none except for the mistaken idea, common to so many gardeners, that anyone can have a wild garden and that the growing of woodland plants, or arctic-alpine ones, or those of the seashore is as easy as growing iris or phlox.

Actually wild gardening needs more study and observation of native plants in their haunts than almost any other type of conventional gardening. Most wild plants resent being moved in their maturity, and some of them resent being moved at all —like the trailing arbutus, the pink lady's-slipper, and the bearberry. Such plants, and scores of other delightful wildlings only slightly less resentful of being moved, demand special conditions of growth, special soil preferences, freedom from wind, shade requirements, and most of all the tiny micro-organisms found in most forest floor humus, in bog mosses, or on the bleak summits of mountains above timber line.

Few can hope to imitate all these widely different types of natural environment, which brings us at once to the question of what type of wild garden one can have. *Wild garden* to most means a shady glade where one can naturalize native plants. But that is only one type of wild garden, and even this will be dictated by the kind of shade you have or can make. Some trees, and their density in the canopy, will make a forest floor so dark that only certain types of wild flowers can be grown under them. This is particularly true of heavy coniferous forests of spruce and fir common in northern New England.

Other forest types, such as the beech-birch-maple which occupy thousands of square miles just south of the great coniferous forests of the north, have a forest floor with more light, but it is still relatively dark and best suited to wildlings that are also quite tolerant of shade.

Still further south, especially along the coastal plain, there are huge areas covered by the typical oak-hickory-sassafras type of forest with a much more open canopy, almost exclusively filtered sunlight, and hence a forest floor lighter than any of the types mentioned above.

Unfortunately, because of the ravages of early forest lumbering, few of us will have any of these forest types in an untouched state. We must, in other words, use second- or third-growth forest with all the miscellaneous tree types that come up in such places. It takes only a few weeks to clear-cut a considerable area of forest, but nearly two hundred years to replace not only the trees, but the incredible alchemy of nature's bequest to the forest floor. Fungi and bacteria, both microscopic organisms of decay, need the kind of moisture found in the humus or duff of a virgin forest.

Depending on the depth of that humus, there is little or no

mineral soil in the surface layer of most forests. Taking a plant from such an environment is a very different matter from moving phlox or iris from one bed to another, for in the latter case ordinary garden soil contains only a fraction of humus, probably not 5% by weight. But the litter even from a relatively poor forest will be 90% humus, and 100% from good sites.

Such forest humus will hold ten times its own weight in water and often more, but few ordinary garden soils will hold more than 15–30% of water. These contrasts simply point up the vastly different conditions which dominate the cultivation of wild plants, from those used for ordinary garden flowers. It points also to the reason for so many failures by "flower lovers" who dig up a wildling from its natural home and doom it to death through ignorance of these simple principles.

There is, too, the very definite restriction that a good many wild flowers will grow best only if there is a definite amount of soil acidity—often quite a lot of it. Their culture without this is hopeless, but fortunately this is one of the easiest of the factors of the environment to control as we shall see later on.

From the beginning of this chapter, but without once using the word you have been reading pure *ecology*. There is no term so simple and so important to the wild gardener. The scientists include within the word ecology the total impact of the environment, and plant or animal accommodation to it. For us it means moisture, shade, temperature, soil conditions, microorganisms, competition between the plants, methods of reproduction—in other words, the complete homelife of the plant. Ecology, after all, is a comparatively new term from the Greek for *knowledge* of the *house,* that is, study of the environment; but the principles of it are as old as man. The first primitive tillers of the soil were ecologists even if they did not know it. It is impossible to become a successful wild gardener without becoming a pretty good amateur ecologist.

ACIDITY AND ALKALINITY

Most ordinary garden flowers have considerable ability to grow in average garden soils, whether neutral, slightly acid, or slightly alkaline. But many wildlings appear to have such a preference for certain degrees of acidity or alkalinity that we must not only know these preferences, but know something about the methods of determining the degree of acidity and alkalinity in soil samples and also how to modify these to suit one's needs.

The chemistry of what lies behind the acidity and alkalinity of soils is a complicated story far too long for this book. Fortunately for wild gardeners there is a very simple short-cut to these complexities which anyone can easily apply by following the directions below.

Pure distilled water is neither acid nor alkaline, but neutral —hence its use in batteries. But it is very rare in nature because rain water, sea water, and soil water have a tendency to absorb various substances which may make them alkaline like sea water or highly acid as in bog water. The concentration of acidity or alkalinity in most soils is spoken of by the experts as its hydrogen-ion concentration. Such a term does not even need a definition in a book like this, for these experts have a symbol for hydrogen-ion concentration which is simply pH. You will find pH in all sorts of government bulletins, in garden books, and in many of the better catalogs. What exactly does it mean to us?

Soils and, of course, soil moisture all have what is called a definite pH value, and so do many other things like the ashes from a pipe or cigarette, beer, tea, urine, blood, and saliva. To measure that value there are several simple devices on the market, and any good wild gardener should get one of them, know how to use it, and interpret its readings. All of them measure pH in terms of the departure from neutral (that is, distilled water) of the substance you are measuring. The scale of pH values is simplicity itself, so far as the wild gardener is concerned.

pH VALUES

Acid	*Neutral: Neither Acid Nor Alkaline*	*Alkaline*
4 5 6	7	8 9

The full scale actually goes from 1 to 12, but only that part of it from 4 to about 8 or 9 is necessary in testing any soil in which plants will grow. The exact significance of these numbers and their use in this and many other books is as follows:

pH4. *Very acid.* Found only in peat bogs, generally covered with sphagnum moss and in the undecomposed duff under coniferous trees. Such a soil will not grow ordinary garden plants but is demanded by some wild flowers such as pink lady's-slipper, the pitcher-plant, the trailing arbutus, etc.

pH 5. *Acid.* Found in upland peaty soils, rotted wood, in some pine-barren soils and often in garden or field soils that have had repeated applications of commercial fertilizers, without liming in recent years. Common wild plants of such regions are the bearberry, most azaleas and rhododendrons.

pH 6. *Slightly acid.* Ordinary garden soils, and many in the upper decomposed layer of woods soils, both in non-limestone areas. It includes many garden soils in which manure or fertilizers have been used but little or no lime. This and the next include hosts of wild flowers and practically all ordinary garden flowers.

pH 7. *Neutral.* Here come, with pH 6, most ordinary garden soils, and pH 7 is usually without much significance to the wild gardener. All plants in this book without any pH number attached to them are considered as being within this range, and hence in no need of particular specifications as to acidity or alkalinity. Fortunately this comprises most of the plants in the book.

pH 8. *Alkaline.* Found only in salt marshes, sand dunes along the seashore (not interior dunes), and heavily limestone regions; also in some mild alkali deserts in the west.

pH 9. *Very alkaline.* Of no significance to the wild gardener unless he is cultivating plants of the alkali deserts of the far west. No ordinary garden plants and no woodland plants will grow in soils of pH 8 or pH 9.

There is often a tendency to refine the simple categories above to the confusion of the amateur and without much help to the experts. You will, for instance, see in some publications formulas like pH 4.7 or pH 5.3, etc. The attempt to subdivide the pH values into decimal places may be essential in medicine and some manufacturing operations (beer, for instance), but it is unnecessary for our purposes and will be ignored here. If you find such figures in other books or bulletins a safe rule would be to assign all such decimal readings to the next category of whole numbers, above or below. Hence pH 5.3 would be pH 5 and pH 4.7 would also be pH 5. If the reading happened to be pH 4.4 it would be pH 4.

In other words, some wild plants, like their garden relatives, have a considerable degree of tolerance and, so long as the soil is definitely acid, they will often grow about as well in pH 4 as pH 5. There is hence little need, except in very rare cases, to subdivide the scale into relatively meaningless decimal places.

To determine these pH values, the experts, especially in medicine and industry, have an elaborate electric instrument, the potentiometer, which reads on a dial to the exact pH value, often in hundredths of a degree. Such refinements are luckily quite unnecessary here and any one of half a dozen soil testing kits will do the job. All of them depend upon the ability of a chemical solution, furnished with the kit, to become a certain color in the presence of a minute bit of soil that is tested. A color scale, with pH values attached to it, will give an almost instantaneous reading of acidity or alkalinity. The kits differ slightly in the technique of usage, but all of them come with directions. The author has made thousands of such tests and the only warning not usually found in the directions is never let cigarette or pipe ashes get into your sample, and never touch the soil you are testing with bare fingers. Both ashes and perspiration are definitely alkaline!

All the plants in which acidity or alkalinity is significant will be indicated by these pH numbers. All others, without numbers, will tolerate a considerable range of acidity or alkalinity, usually between pH 6 to above pH 7, and in some cases nearly to pH 8. They do not need to worry the wild gardener —at least as to this factor.

DOES IT PAY TO CHANGE YOUR SOIL?

This is largely an economic and common-sense problem. If you want to grow a few acid-tolerant plants but live in a limestone region, it can easily be done and relatively inexpensively. But to convert such a predominately alkaline soil to an acid one would be obviously foolish on any considerable scale, say, an acre or two. In the latter case you would not be a good wild gardener or ecologist, but someone with more money than brains, for it would involve a lot of costly soil moving. But acid-tolerant* plants can be grown in a limestone region, on a small scale, by following the directions below.

For a small bed or container it is quite easy to change the pH value and at the same time make a mixture that will have the right texture for most woodland plants. To make a bushel of finished soil use:

1 part clean sharp sand (not sea sand unless all salt has been removed by thorough washing.)

1 part ordinary garden loam.

3 parts of acid peat (available from many dealers.)

Mix these ingredients thoroughly and then test the mixture with your soil kit. If it reads pH 6 and you want it to be pH 4, take about ¾ pound of aluminum sulfate to each bushel of your mixture. See that the aluminum sulfate is thoroughly mixed with your sample and then test it again. Keep on adding small amounts of aluminum sulfate until your mixture tests as near pH 4 as you can get it. The exact amount of aluminum sulfate that you will need cannot be specified, as the pH of your original mixture will vary and it takes more aluminum sulfate to change a heavy loam than a sandy one.

If, on the other hand, your original mixture tests at pH 6 and you want it to be pH 7 or 8 (for alkali-tolerant plants), then to each bushel of your original mixture add not more than one ounce of hydrated lime, which should be thoroughly mixed with your soil. Keep on testing this and adding minute amounts of lime until the

* *Acid-tolerant* and *alkali-tolerant* are terms used throughout this book to avoid such doubtful designations as acid-loving, lime-loving, limestone plants, lime-haters, etc. All such anthropomorphic terms imply a considerable ignorance of ecology. It is scientifically correct to say that certain plants grow in acid or alkali soils. They grow there not because they "like" or "hate" such situations but because they must.

treated mixture reaches pH 7 or 8. If you use ground limestone it will take a little more to get the same effect.

These two simple procedures will make you master of the acid and alkali problems in the cultivation of all wild flowers that have special requirements. You can practically "make" your soil to suit your requirements—at least on a relatively small scale. Sometimes, if you are lucky, you may get humus from the woods or from a dealer and save most of the trouble of mixing, or maybe you have a natural woodland. However, such material should always be tested and treated like your "made" soil if it does not come up to your specifications.

Such a tested mixture, whether natural humus or your "made" soil should be at least 18 inches deep for most wild perennials, and about 2½ feet deep for azaleas and rhododendrons. To make room for it all old soil should be dug out to the required depth. Fill in your tested mixture and wet it down. Do not use tap water if it tests (as many hard waters do) more highly alkaline than you want your mixture to be. Use rain water for the first time or two. Later on rainfall should take care of water requirements. If you are growing the plants in a pot or tub indoors you may have to catch enough rain water for their needs. It is not safe to use village or city tap water unless its pH value is very near that of your prepared soil. Your soil kit will test tap water as well as soil samples.

As to the yearly maintenance of such made soils or any other, you can top-dress them with small amounts of aluminum sulfate for acid sites, or lime for alkaline situations. By yearly testing and the addition of the required chemicals you can keep your wild plants in a perfect environment so far as acidity and alkalinity is concerned. Liming will usually not need replenishment more often than every third or fourth year.

MOISTURE

You cultivate ordinary garden soil not only to keep weeds under control but to conserve soil moisture. The theory behind the latter is that your hoeing or cultivation makes the top-most layer of soil a so-called dust mulch. These dry fine particles of cultivated soil tend to blanket the normal evaporation of soil moisture from uncultivated areas. A simple illustration of this interference with the usual action of water rising by capillarity (which happens in all garden and farm soils) is your failure to make a drop of water mix with cocoa without stirring it.

The dust mulch at the top of all cultivated garden soils breaks capillarity just as cocoa "repels" the drop of water. A good test of the theory is to put a drop or two of water on a saucer, place a lump of sugar on it and see how quickly the water will rise in the lump—almost instantaneously. The reason why it rises in the sugar and will not in cocoa or cultivated soil is that the particles are too fine in the latter and hence prevent capillarity from working as it normally does in all uncultivated soils.

What, you will be asking, has all this to do with wild gardening? It is fundamental, for no wild garden should ever be cultivated. Never hoe it or use one of the many scratching devices that flood the market. Your aim in the wild garden is not to conserve moisture by cultivating the top-most layer of soil but to *leave it alone.* Who in a natural forest ever heard of "cultivating" the forest floor? But it is precisely in such places that our beautiful and most shy wild flowers flourish. No one is conserving their soil moisture.

Where, then, do they get it, and how is the wild gardener to be sure his site will be as close an imitation of the forest floor as possible? The answer, as in so many problems of the woodland garden, is pure ecology. The composition of most forest surface soils is nearly pure vegetable matter. Its moisture-holding capacity is ten times, and often thirty times, that of any ordinary garden (that is, mineral) soil. Hence it holds moisture and makes an ideal medium for the flourishing not only of wild flowers, but for the micro-organisms upon which so many of them depend for their best growth.

Such soil conditions are never found under isolated trees in a lawn, only slightly in thin sparse forests or woodlots, but nearly always under the natural canopy of a mature forest. These facts make it obvious that you cannot have a successful woodland garden under one or two or even a handful of trees. They will not make the right conditions of shade and soil moisture. In such places, as we shall see in subsequent chapters, it is possible to naturalize many less-demanding wild flowers, some of them most desirable, but it is no place for those wildlings whose home is the forest and naturally resent any environment that does not remind them that you are a true wild gardener and ecologist.

What, you will ask, must I do about weeds in the wild garden if I must not cultivate it? The answer to that perfectly natural question is go into the interior of any mature forest —and it is always weedless! If you have weeds it probably means your wild garden is not yet really wild, does not yet quite imitate the ecological conditions of the forest, and hence weeds get a start. If they do there is nothing for it but to hand-pull them. Under no circumstances should you hoe them out or cultivate the soil in any way.

In most areas east of the Alleghenies the rain and snow will provide all the moisture needed by the forest and its wild flowers and for your woodland garden. But rainfall decreases rather rapidly as one goes west of this range and, wherever the annual rainfall is less than 20 inches, woodland gardens are not advised unless you have ample water of the right pH and are prepared to use it. Rainfall of less than 20 inches begins at approximately eastern North Dakota, Nebraska, Kansas, Oklahoma, and Texas. West of this, woodland gardens, except in the Rockies and the Pacific Coast, are impossible. Both the latter areas lie outside the scope of this book, for both the plants and climate differ too much to be included here.

HOW TO START

Given the proper conditions of shade, soil moisture, acidity, and alkalinity, what is the best way to start a woodland garden? Should one collect the plants from the wild, buy them from a dealer, or try raising his own from seeds. The latter is undoubtedly to be preferred and it is far cheaper than purchasing plants. But it is slow, often needs skills that are hard to come by, and in some cases impossible. Wherever, in future chapters, growing your own from seed seems advisable, directions for it are given.

Otherwise purchasing them from a dealer or collecting them from the wild are your only sources. As to the latter there is needed a serious warning. Many so-called flower lovers show their fondness for nature by ignorant destruction of it. Certain wild flowers should never be picked, let alone any attempt be made to dig them out, whether dormant or not. Some of our choicest woodland plants are on the way to becoming extinct because of the well-meant but stupid depredations of "wild flower enthusiasts." No censure is too severe for such people and no law too drastic. Generally they seem immune to both. Who has not seen of a spring week-end thousands of bedraggled wild flowers, their parched cups nodding from car windows, limp in heat and the fumes of gasoline. Such an ecological insult is not the way to show your love of nature, nor will it ever stock a woodland garden.

If woodland garden plants are to be dug up a few simple rules should be followed:

1. Never dig one out that is rare in your vicinity.
2. Never dig anything out when it is in full flower. (This will mean marking the plant with a stake and coming back to it when it is dormant; that is, after all leaves have died down for the season.)
3. Be sure to get all roots (often they are quite extensive) and as much of the native soil as you can carry, preferably in a "sod" or clump in which the roots are relatively undisturbed.
4. Try not to dig on a windy day or after a long drought.
5. Do not leave dug plants out of the ground any longer than necessary, never as long as overnight.
6. See to it that the conditions of shade, moisture, and acidity are provided for in accordance with the suggestions earlier in this chapter.
7. Water newly set plants for the first week or two. Rainfall should take care of them afterward.
8. Before digging or planting anything, look it up in the index to find out whether its culture is all but impossible, or whether it has some unsuspected requirements too detailed to be mentioned here. These are noted for all critical plants.
9. Do not expect to succeed with plants from cool, moist high elevations if they are moved to the warm, dry lowlands of the coastal plain, and *vice versa*. Notes in the following chapters will give this detail for all plants that need it.
10. Be alert for the possible destruction of neighboring woodlands due to real estate "improvements" or road making. The transplanting of such threatened plants to a woodland garden may be the only means of saving them.

WINTER CARE

Autumn leaf-fall brings nostalgic memories of cool nights, open fires, and the peculiar, pungent fragrant smoke of burning leaves. Nothing could be worse for the wild garden than the burning of leaves. Again let us take a final visit to the forest and see what nature is doing with the annual deposition of that most precious of all forest assets, humus. If there are oaks the dead leaves will be adding acidity to the forest floor, perhaps just enough to correct what has been lost by leaching. If it is a coniferous forest, and hence with no real leaf-fall, the slow dropping of hundreds of tiny needles all through the year will be adding even more acidity. Nor is this all.

Some time ago the writer stood in the rain in such a forest and caught the drip from twigs and bark to test it for acidity. It was more acid than the forest floor itself, which means that nature by leaf-fall and run-off from the trees is annually building up the humus layer. It is protecting the place where forest tree seeds will germinate and wild flowers thrive and will do so forever if only fire is kept out. If fire comes the disaster is complete, even if not a tree is killed, for so-called ground fires change the forest floor from an acid or partly acid environment to a drastic alkaline one.

The implications of this are obvious. Keep fire out of the woodland garden and allow leaf-fall to stay where it is. If wind is likely to carry off the crop of fallen leaves it is wise to hold them in place by chicken wire and a few battens. If your canopy does not contain species with acid-forming capacity such as maples, ash, linden, and many others, it is advisable to bring in oak leaves. The droppings from any pines, spruces, firs, or hemlock, especially if they are mixed with other trees, will usually take care of acid requirements.

In the spring allow the dead leaves to rot away. They will be doing for the wild garden what they do in the forest—adding humus, making the right environment for those shy and elusive woodland plants that are perfectly hardy in their own forests but need devoted attention when moved to your woodland garden. The best of them will be found in the next chapter.

Plants for the Woodland Garden

CHAPTER II

G*IVEN* the natural or made conditions outlined in the last chapter, there are still things to be thought of before doing any planting. In nearly all second- or third-growth forests, as most of us will have to deal with, there is almost surely an undergrowth of shrubs. This makes a thicket-like growth, often nearly impenetrable, and no place for the naturalization of wildlings.

Clear all such growth out of the site of the wild garden. Often merely cutting such shrubs at the ground-level, when in full leaf, will be enough. But some of them will sprout from the roots the next spring, and these shoots should also be cut off while in full leaf. Keep this up until you have killed off most of the thicket shrubs, but leave the dead roots in the ground to decay. Dig out only the most persistent

PLATE 3

Joseph R. Swain

MAYAPPLE
Podophyllum peltatum

Lawrence D. Hiett

BLOODROOT
Sanguinaria canadensis

Russell Tinling Pansie

CALIFORNIA POPPY
Eschscholtzia californica

PLATE 4

Harold D. Roberts

GUMBO-LILY
Nuttallia decapetala

Harold D. Roberts

ROCKY MOUNTAIN BEEPLANT
Peritoma serrulatum

Hugo H. Schroder

LARGER BLUE FLAG
Iris versicolor

PLATE 5

Harold D. Roberts

WESTERN WALLFLOWER
Cheirinia aspera

Walter Henricks Hodge

FRINGED MILKWORT
Triclisperma paucifolia

Russell Tinling Pansie

BIRDSFOOT VIOLET
Viola pedata

Russell Tinling Pansie

COMMON SPIDERWORT
Tradescantia virginiana

Walter Henricks Hodge

VENUS-FLYTRAP
Dionaea muscipula

shrubs, of which there should not be too many after a year or two of cutting all leafy shoots at the ground level.

Never use any chemical weed killers to clear out this shrubby growth. It must be removed unless you are lucky enough to have wild azalea or rhododendrons on the site. These, of course, should be treasured, and if you have none, occasional planted islets of azalea and rhododendron or mountain laurel will tremendously enhance your woodland garden.

Another and quite important feature is the path if the garden is extensive enough to need one. Make paths as narrow and winding as possible, for the object is merely to get about in the garden, without making ugly gashes through your woodland that let in too much wind and maybe too much sunshine. The woodland garden cannot be too secluded and should never be subject to the hot, drying winds that have blown over paved streets or cement sidewalks. The ideal site is a woodland surrounded by lawn, or at least with a lawn between it and the prevailing summer wind. Native woodland plants can stand any degree of winter cold, but very little of the hot, drying winds of summer.

To prevent too much summer wind sweeping through your woodland garden, it is often wise to plant a screen of shrubs between it and the prevailing summer wind. These winds, east of the Alleghenies, are generally south or southwest, and they are, especially if coinciding with a drought, far more damaging than any amount of winter cold.

If your site is a sloping one and faces towards the north or northeast, wind may be no problem. If it faces south or southwest, your precautions should be that much more effective. Heat conditions on a south slope are vastly different from those on a north one, and the shrubby screen for such a south-facing woodland garden must be adequate. It should keep out most summer winds, and even those of May and June when many of the spring-blooming woodland plants are at their most beautiful but also their most vulnerable stage. Best of all is a high evergreen hedge of arbor-vitae or hemlock, but both are rather expensive.

When it comes to the actual planting of any of the species in the list that follows there are a few things to remember. Most woodland wild flowers grow in clumps or patches. Such groups may contain from three or four plants to, more often, scores, and sometimes there are "sheets of bloom" where several hundred individual plants are crowded into what the ecologists call an "association." These natural arrangements make the best guide as to how many of a single species you want in each group. Wild flowers are better planted in groups, of whatever size you choose, than singly. Many of them are shy bloomers and no woodland garden will ever be a blaze of color such as you may easily obtain with many ordinary garden flowers. Hence it is better to plant wild flowers in patches of a dozen or so, not only for appearance but because they often act as though they liked to be grown with their own kind rather than with strangers. Also, individual plants in a woodland garden are apt to look spotty. A very few, like some people, are natural solitaries and should be planted alone. All such are noted at the proper place.

WOODLAND PLANTS

There are only forty-one genera of woodland plants in the list below. That, of course, does not comprise one tenth of all the plants that grow in our woodlands. But it does include most of those that are likely to be useful to the amateur, and all of them are available from dealers in native plants. A good many of the rarer woodland plants are not carried by any dealer and even the seeds of many of them are not to be found in any catalog. For practical reasons such plants are excluded from the list below, and all woodland orchids are found in a special chapter devoted to them. Also excluded, because of the difficulty of cultivating them, are a few plants that will be found in the last chapter.

ALUMROOT

Those that remain in the list below can be grown with comparative ease in the woodland garden if careful attention has been paid to the directions already outlined. Because the time of bloom is so important in planning any garden, it is given for all the plants mentioned, with the understanding that the dates given are for the latitude of New York City. North of this and at higher elevations they will bloom later, and south of it considerably earlier.

All the plants in the list that demand special conditions of acidity will have a pH value attached to them. They should be grown in soils such as described in Chapter I, made to fit these requirements. (See Chapter I for details.) All others, without a pH value are tolerant of any good humus soil, but it is not recommended that you grow them in ordinary garden loam. Those without a pH value are mostly in the range of pH 6–7. All are perennials unless otherwise designated.

ALUMROOT. *Heuchera americana.* A wand-like plant with mostly basal, heart-shaped, mottled, bronzy leaves that are often evergreen. Flowering stalk 12–20 inches high, the greenish-purple flowers in a lax cluster, mostly in June. It is related to coral-bells of the garden. A wild relative is *Heuchera villosa,* which is lower and has white flowers. Both are easy to grow in humus either in deep shade or in filtered sunlight.

ANEMONE. *Anemone quinquefolia,* pH 5–6. A delicate little perennial, shy as to bloom, avoiding windy places and completely dying down to the ground when through flowering. Never more than 6–8 inches high, this wood anemone, or windflower as it is often called, rises from a slender, easily broken rootstock and should be handled with care. Leaves divided, the lobes wedge-shaped. Flowers solitary, white, very fragile, mostly in early May. The plant is almost useless unless planted in masses. A close relative of it will be found in this list at WINDFLOWER, a much more hardy plant.

Related to *Anemone quinquefolia,* but very different from it are *Anemone canadensis* and *A. cylindrica.* Both are stout perennials with erect stiff stems, 12–20 inches high, rather coarse, divided leaves and solitary green or white flowers. Both are much easier to grow than *A. quinquefolia* and need no special pH conditions. Both of them flower in late May or early June. For a related species of *Anemone* see the pasqueflower in Chapter III devoted to plants of thickets and open places.

BANEBERRY. *Actaea.* There are two common species of baneberry in the woods of eastern North America, both of them worth growing in the woodland garden. *Actaea alba,* pH 6–7, is a stouter plant than *A. rubra* (pH 5–6), with thickish stalks to its white fruit. In *A. rubra* the stalks to its red fruit are almost thread-like. Both species have relatively inconspicuous, small, white flowers in a long-stalked, terminal cluster. They are much more showy in fruit than in flower, and prefer deep shade to sunshine. Both of them flower about mid-May and are about 12–18 inches high.

BELLWORT. *Uvularia.* Delicate woodland plants of eastern North America, often called merrybells because of their nodding, bell-shaped, green or yellow flowers which are often half hidden among the smooth, stalkless leaves. Three species are worth a place in the wild garden, and all of them are from 8–15 inches tall. The showiest is *Uvularia grandiflora,* pH 7–8, with yellow, mostly terminal flowers, and leaves in which the stem passes through the blade. *Uvularia perfoliata,* pH 5–6, also has the leaf-blade pierced by the stem, but with smaller, yellow flowers. *Uvularia sessilifolia,* with straw-colored flowers, is the least attractive of the lot. All bloom in May or early June and, if given the right conditions are easy to grow.

BLOODROOT. *Sanguinaria canadensis,* pH 6–7. This is probably the most popular of all woodland garden plants since it transplants easily, propagates readily, and if once established will make delightful patches in a few years. The plant is scarcely over 7–8 inches high, and in late April or early May the rolled leaf breaks through the ground, tightly clasping the flower bud. Flowers solitary, usually with 8 waxy-white petals, often 1½–2 inches wide, very showy, but extremely fragile and hence useless for picking. There is a double-flowered variety said to be natural and originating in some woods at Ann Arbor, Michigan. The double-flowered variety sets no seeds, must therefore be purchased from a dealer, and is a better plant for the wild garden than the common sort.

While bloodroot can be dug from the wild almost in full flower and still survive, it is better to wait until the much expanded leaf, which follows flower withering, is itself dying down. In some states bloodroot has become so scarce that no one should dig it out. The best, if the slowest method of propagation in that case, is by seeds. Collect fresh seed and sow at once in a mixture of half humus and half sand, covered with about ½ inch of shredded sphagnum moss. Seeds will not germinate until the following spring. Division of the roots can be made any time after flowering. See Color Plate 3.

Blue Cohosh. *Caulophyllum thalictroides.* A stout perennial, 2–3 feet high, the much-divided leaves with the ultimate segments suggesting the meadow rue. A single leaf is borne about halfway up the smooth stem, but close up to the flower cluster there may be another and much smaller leaf. Flowers few, in a loose terminal cluster, greenish-purple, with a yellow center and not very conspicuous. It is followed by a few, handsome, cherry-sized, blue and showy fruit, for which the plant is well worth cultivation. Flowers in late April or early May, the fruits ripening and most conspicuous in June–July. Needs a dark, shady place.

Clintonia. There are two species of Clintonia, both of which grow naturally in mountain woods or even in sphagnum bogs in the far north, and are best grown away from the heat of the coastal plain. *Clintonia borealis,* the bluebead or corn-lily, needs a pH of about 5, fairly deep shade, considerable moisture, and grows naturally in moist rock crevices. It is 8–15 inches high, has basal leaves suggesting the lily-of-the-valley, and a terminal cluster of 3–8, greenish-yellow, lily-like flowers that are scarcely ½ inch long, in May, followed by bright blue, football-shaped fruits, not over ½ inch long. Its close relative, *Clintonia umbellulata,* pH 6, has more numerous, white flowers and black, shiny fruit. Neither species should be attempted in open dry woods. In nature they are among our rarer wild flowers, too precious to be wasted on unsuitable sites.

COLUMBINE. *Aquilegia canadensis.* A woodland perennial, 12–30 inches high, the leaves mostly basal and divided into several segments; also a few stem leaves that are much smaller. Flowers nodding, with five conspicuous, hollow, spurs, generally scarlet or red, but also with yellow segments, and one of our most showy spring wildflowers, blooming mostly in early May. It does not like dry, open woods, but will grow in partial or deep shade if the site is moist. Its stoutish rootstock may mislead the amateur into assuming it is easy to transplant. Actually it needs considerable care, especially if the site is too dry and windy. A much more showy columbine, *Aquilegia coerulea,* from the Rocky Mountains, has larger, blue flowers and is much more easily grown. It needs some moisture and partial shade, but will often grow well in ordinary garden soil. It thrives in the woodland garden, blooms in June and is 2–3 feet high. (See Color Plate 1.)

CULVER'S-ROOT. *Veronicastrum virginicum* (often sold as *Veronica virginica*). Not many woodland plants flower as late as midsummer, or do well in open filtered sunlight, but Culver's-root does both. It is a stout herb, 3–5 feet high, its narrow, willow-like, toothed leaves arranged in isolated clusters on the stem. Flowers minute, crowded in dense, terminal, spire-like clusters, the plants hence showy and most welcome at a season when most woodland plants have long passed their blooming periods. Culver's-root is easy to grow in any humus-containing soil and often grows wild on our central prairies. It was once and is still by some thought to have medicinal value, hence its other name of Culver's-physic, or *Leptandra,* under which name it may be listed in old catalogs.

DOG'S-TOOTH VIOLET. *Erythronium americanum* pH 5–6, often called trout-lily or leopard-lily, the latter because of its brown-mottled, mostly basal leaves. It is one of our most desirable woodland plants, generally grows in extensive patches and is best planted in reasonably numerous groups (10–20 plants). Flowers solitary, terminal, yellow, showy, on a stalk not over 8 inches high; early May. The plant grows from a deep rootstock, and attempts to dig it from the wild must be deep enough (3–5 inches) to get below this and its attached roots. It prefers moist to dry sites, and a closely related plant, *Erythronium albidum* pH 6–7 with less mottled leaves and white flowers, is easier to grow than the common dog's-tooth violet.

There are many other species of *Erythronium* from the Rocky Mountains, the Cascades, and the Sierra Nevada of California, but most of them are a bit difficult to establish in the east. Many of them are far more showy than those found in the east. Among the best of them and most likely to succeed are:

Erythronium californicum. .... Cream-yellow
Erythronium grandiflorum. .... Yellow
Erythronium purdyi. .... White, with yellow center

DUTCHMAN'S BREECHES. *Dicentra cucullaria,* pH 6–7. In moist, rocky, woods, usually out of the wind, there grows this lacy-leaved perennial which bears small, fragile, twin-spurred, cream-yellow flowers. It is one of our most delicate wild flowers, wild cousin to the garden bleeding-heart, and only 6–10 inches high. Soon after its May blooming flowers have withered, the leaves also die down so that there is little or no evidence of it by midsummer. Propagation is by the separation of its tuber-like collection of white, small grain-like roots, and it must be done when the plant is dormant. A close relative, the squirrel-corn, *Dicentra canadensis* pH 6–7, is lower, even more delicate, and much less common as a wild plant. Neither is likely to do well on the coastal plain.

Still another relative is the wild bleeding-heart, *Dicentra eximia,* pH 5–6. It has the same fern-like foliage, grows 8–15 inches high, but has pink flowers that bloom from May to midsummer. It is much showier than the Dutchman's breeches and easier to grow, since it often thrives in half shade in ordinary garden soil. It is more closely related to the common bleeding-heart of the gardens, *Dicentra spectabilis,* than to the Dutchman's breeches.

DWARF CORNEL. *Cornus canadensis,* pH 4–5. This is really a very dwarf shrub, never over 6 inches high, and in spite of its size closely related to the flowering dogwood. It has a basal rosette of bluntish leaves, from which spring the greenish inconspicuous flowers which would pass notice except for the white, conspicuous bracts very like those of the flowering dogwood, but smaller. May-blooming. Not to be attempted on the warm coastal plain, as its natural habitat is cool mountain woods, or in cold bogs covered with sphagnum moss, where its bright red berries are as showy as its flowers. The dwarf cornel, which is sometimes called bunchberry, makes a fine groundcover if the site is cool and moist enough. Propagate by separating its sod-like clumps, when dormant, or seed from the ripe berries will germinate if planted ¼ inch deep in a mixture of ¾ sand and ¼ chopped sphagnum. They must be kept moist and acid, and will not germinate until the next spring. (See Color Plate 12 (as bunchberry).)

False Solomon's-seal. *Smilacina racemosa.* An easily grown perennial in almost any woods soil (and often in others) if given partial shade. It tolerates lack of moisture better than most woodland plants, but is not very handsome or showy. It grows from 16 to 30 inches high, has a wand-like stem, rather coarse leaves and a terminal, branched cluster of minute, white flowers, followed by speckled, red berries. Blooms in late May or early June; fruits ripe in August. Its long rootstock easily separated for propagating.

Ferns. No woodland garden would be complete without a liberal use of ferns, and many sites chosen for one will already have a natural growth of native ferns. If there are none you can easily dig them out of the woods in the late fall, and most of the kinds worth growing will thrive in any good woods soil with a pH 6–7. If there are no ferns in your vicinity from which to stock your woodland garden, they can be easily purchased from all dealers in wild garden material. Among the best for a woodland garden are:

Maidenhair. *Adiantum pedatum,* 12–18 inches.
Lady fern. *Athyrium filix-femina,* 12–30 inches.
Male fern. *Dryopteris filix-mas,* 9–18 inches.
Cinnamon fern. *Osmunda cinnamomea,* 24–36 inches.
Christmas fern. *Polystichum acrostichoides,* 9–18 inches.
Virginia chain. *Woodwardia virginica,* 24–36 inches.

There are, of course, many other native ferns, but these six will give most amateurs all the choice they need; they are of relatively easy culture and all of them are readily available from dealers. All of them need shade, and moist sites are better than dry ones.

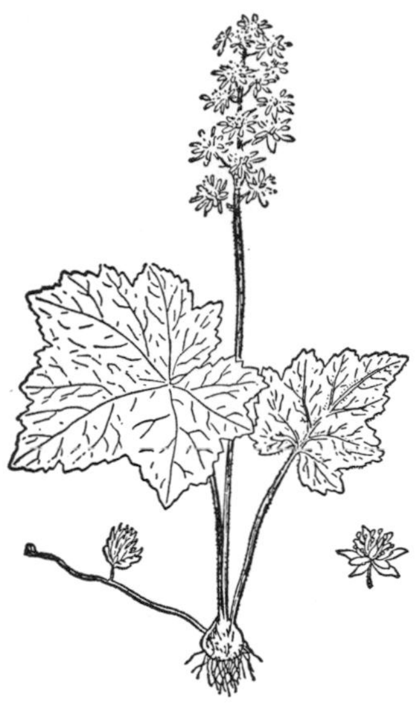

FOAM-FLOWER

FOAM-FLOWER. *Tiarella cordifolia,* pH 5–6. Planted in masses the foam-flower looks just like that. It has basal, more or less heart-shaped leaves, and a flower cluster that stands above them, the whole plant scarcely 8 inches high. The flowers are small, cream-white, but crowded in the cluster and suggesting flecks of foam on the forest floor. The plant is a perennial, easily transplanted when dormant, but is far better suited to cool northern woods than to warm dry ones. It blooms in May.

GALAX. *Galax aphylla.* pH 5. Few of our woodland plants have evergreen leaves, which makes galax a fine groundcover in rich, cool woods. Their almost universal use for funeral wreaths need not deter the wild gardener from growing this fine plant from the mountains of Virginia, North Carolina, and northern Georgia. It is perfectly hardy up to New York and Connecticut, preferably away from the Coast. The heart-shaped leaves are lustrous-green in deep shade and in summer, but become bronzy if grown in partial shade, and often more so in winter. Like its close relative *Shortia* it has white flowers, in a spire-like cluster that may be 10–15 inches long, blooming in late May or early June. It is not one of the easiest wild flowers to establish, but the plants can be divided in early spring, and in a suitably acid, moist site should do well. It thrives under the shade of rhododendrons and azaleas in its mountain haunts, where it is very common.

GAY-WINGS. *Polygala paucifolia* pH 5–6. This delicate little perennial is fairly hard to get established in the wild garden. It grows scarcely over 6 inches high, with half-evergreen, small leaves that become bronzy late in the fall. Its chief charm is the small, purple, fringed (rarely white) flowers that have two fringed wing-like petals. The plant tends to sprawl, and its prostrate stems, with their few attending roots, are difficult to dig out without courting failure. More certain is making cuttings in June, which should be dipped into a hormone-like solution that promotes root growth. Such cuttings, planted in a mixture of half sand and half acid peat, will root if kept moist and in the shade, so that the young plants will be ready to set out the following spring. Most amateurs will prefer to buy rooted plants from a dealer. They bloom in late May or early June, and the plant should not be grown near the warm coastal plain. (See Color Plate 5 (as fringed milkwort).) A relative is *Polygala senega,* the Seneca snakeroot, which is not so showy, has white or greenish-white flowers, and is far easier to grow in partial shade or even in the open, as it grows wild on some of our prairies.

For still a third relative, *Polygala lutea,* see the chapter on swamp, bog, and meadow plants.

GINSENG. *Panax quinquefolium.* Because of the collection of its roots for their supposed medicinal value to the Chinese (mostly superstition), this has become one of our rarest woodland plants. It is still grown commercially, mostly under lath shade, but no one should attempt this without long experience in growing Ginseng and until China is open to free trade. It may be grown in the wild garden in any good woods soil, under natural shade, but neither its foliage nor inconspicuous greenish-white flowers make it an attractive wild garden subject. Grown for interest, and as a rarity, it merits attention, because millions of pounds of its roots have been shipped to China over the years. The root is often forked, when its value is thrice that of an unbranched root. The forked, almost man-shaped root is supposed to promote fertility, which teeming China scarcely needs!

GOLDENSEAL. *Hydrastis canadensis.* This is probably the most valuable of all our native woodland plants and is now most rare due to years of collection of its roots. The roots contain hydrastine, which is of considerable medicinal value. Large commercial plantations of it are grown under lath shade, but its cultivation for profit is not advised, unless one is experienced in its culture. As a wild garden plant it can be grown in any good, woodsy soil, under partial or dense shade, preferably in cool, mountainous sites. It has very large, basal leaves, which are deeply lobed. Flowers greenish-white, inconspicuous, blooming in late April, followed by a head of raspberry-like berries. Plants of it must be purchased, as it is now all but exterminated in the wild.

GOLDTHREAD. *Coptis trifolia.* pH 4–5. The thread-like golden roots of this little perennial suggest its name and also tell us what it likes as to environment. It will not grow well unless the woods soil is full of humus, decidedly acid, moist during the growing season, and cool. If you cannot duplicate such conditions it is better to skip goldthread. It is a slender plant, not over 4–5 inches high, with divided evergreen leaves and small white, rather waxy, but small flowers. It often grows in sphagnum bogs up to the Arctic Circle and should never be grown on the warm coastal plain.

HEPATICA. *Hepatica americana.* pH 5–6. While most people call this favorite spring flower hepatica it is also known as Mayflower, from its blooming early in May (often in April); others call it liver-leaf or liverwort, from the shape of its partly evergreen leaves. These stay green all winter, but send out a new crop after the lavender or pinkish-white flowers have bloomed. It is one of the easier wild flowers to grow and can be dug from the woods anytime, but best when the plant is relatively dormant in autumn. Not over 6–8 inches high. It prefers part shade and will thrive in most woods soil. A close relative, *Hepatica acutiloba,* has pointed leaf lobes instead of rounded ones and generally grows where the soil is about pH 6–7.

JACK-IN-THE-PULPIT. *Arisaema triphyllum.* pH 6–7. Often called Indian turnip (the Indians used it as food, after the bitter, acrid, turnip-like root had been cooked). The plant is 18–30 inches high, the leaves 3-parted, and from among them arises the stalked pulpit or hooded spathe which may be fluted or plain, greenish or reddish-brown, and which encloses the finger-like spadix (Jack) with its almost microscopic flowers. Its scarlet berries, about ½ inch in diameter, are very showy. The plant luxuriates in damp woods, but can be grown in drier sites if there is shade. In digging wild plants (after fruiting time) it is essential to get all of the turnip-like root, which in old plants may be 10–15 inches deep.

A relative of the Jack-in-the-pulpit is the green dragon, *Arisaema dracontium,* pH 5–6. It is often 3 feet high at maturity, and its "pulpit" does not include the long-protruding spadix. It also prefers moist woods and is a little less tolerant of drier sites. Not so handsome as the Jack-in-the-pulpit.

LILY. *Lilium.* A protean group in the native flora and containing some of our most showy wild flowers. Not all of them are woodland plants, and those of moist, open places and thickets should be sought in the chapters devoted to plants of such places. The best lilies for the woodland garden are:

Wood lily. *Lilium philadelphicum.* pH 4–5. A showy lily, 20–36 inches high its leaves in clusters on the stem. Flowers erect, reddish-orange, spotted inside, summer-blooming. It arises from a deep bulb and this must be dug when the plant is becoming dormant. Can be grown in relatively dry woods, in deep or partial shade. Plant the bulbs at least 5–6 inches deep, and it is safer to start with purchased bulbs.

Carolina lily. *Lilium michauxi.* pH 4–5. A southern lily well suited to dry, sandy woods and not to be tried in the cool, moist woods of the mountains. It resembles the Turk's-cap lily (see lilies of moist places in another chapter), but is smaller. Flowers nodding, orange-red but purple-spotted, and very handsome, August-blooming. It is better to start with purchased plants or bulbs, and in some catalogs it may be listed as *Lilium carolinianum.* Plant in fairly open woods as it does not thrive in dense shade.

Gray's lily. *Lilium grayi.* A tall lily, often up to five feet in height in the wild, usually less as cultivated. Sometimes called the bell lily, it has narrow leaves in clusters, and a nodding, bell-shaped deep red flower, plentifully purple-spotted on the inside, generally blooming in late June or

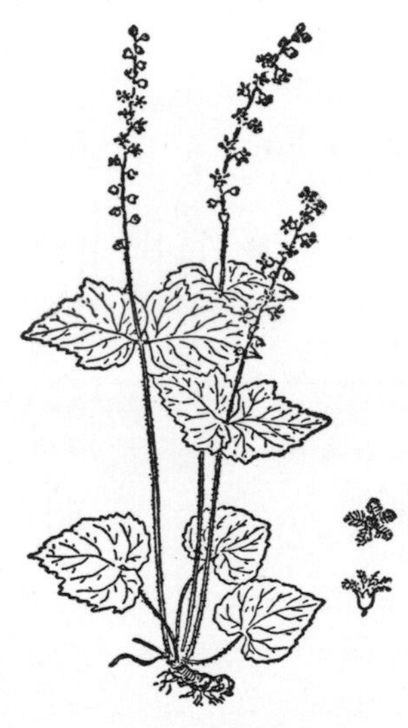

MITREWORT

July. It wants a damp or moist place under partial shade.

MAYAPPLE. *Podophyllum peltatum.* pH 5–6. A gregarious wild flower, mostly growing in fairly large patches and best grown so in the wild garden. The plant is showy with its wax-like, white flower, but in spite of its name, the rootstock, leaves, and seeds are all poisonous. It is 12–18 inches high, May-blooming, followed in August by its handsome, yellow, edible fruit

PLATE 7

Russell Tinling Pansie

BOTTLE GENTIAN
Dasystephana andrewsii

Joseph R. Swain

LARGER YELLOW LADYSLIPPER
Cypripedium calceolus var. *pubescens*

Russell Tinling Pansie

FIREPINK
Silene virginica

Harold D. Roberts

NORTHWESTERN SPRINGBEAUTY
Claytonia lanceolata

Harold D. Roberts

BITTERROOT
Lewisia rediviva

Harold D. Roberts

BLUE FLAX
Linum lewisii

Russell Tinling Pansie

SPOTTED CRANESBILL
Geranium maculatum

Joseph R. Swain

PURPLE LOOSESTRIFE
Lythrum salicaria

Harold D. Roberts

GREAT WILLOWHERB
Chamaenerion spicatum

PLATE 10

Joseph R. Swain

PAINTED WAKEROBIN
Trillium undulatum

Harold D. Roberts

DUNE SANDVERBENA
Abronia maritima

Russell Tinling Pansie

DEERGRASS
Rhexia virginica

(except the seeds). Non-flowering, young plants have a single, much-divided, broad leaf, but the flowering plants have two considerably smaller leaves, from between which arises the practically stalkless flower. Grown best in moist, shady places, and once established its stout rootstocks will soon form a considerable colony. It grows 12–20 inches high, and in the wild is rampant. (See Color Plate 3.)

MITREWORT. *Mitella diphylla.* pH 5–6. Often called bishop's-cap and closely related to the foam-flower, treated earlier in this chapter, but with an interrupted flower cluster which is wand-like and 5–15 inches high. The small flowers are white, blooming in late May or early June, the petals fringed. Grows best in deep, moist, rocky woods.

PARTRIDGEBERRY. *Mitchella repens.* pH 5–6. A prostrate, creeping, vine-like perennial which grows in mats from which arise flowering stalks, 3–4 inches high, crowned with two small, white flowers joined at the base and suggesting the twinflower treated later in this chapter. Flowers bloom in June, followed by the edible, scarlet berries. Partridgeberry is of easy culture in almost any open or shaded woods, and its creeping stem is readily rooted at the joints.

PHLOX. *Phlox.* A predominately American group of plants, many of them contributing to the ancestry of the garden phloxes of today. There are far too many woodland species to include all of them here, but the following are useful in any woodland garden:

Blue phlox. *Phlox divaricata.* pH 6–7. Grows 9–15 inches high, the clustered blue-lavender flowers with the lobes of the corolla notched. Of easy culture in almost any woodsy place, preferably somewhat moist. Blooms in May.

Wild Sweet William. *Phlox maculata.* Erect, 10–20 inches

high, the stiff flower cluster crowded with showy reddish-purple flowers that bloom in June or July. Grows best in moist places under partial shade.

Phlox paniculata. This is the ancestor of many ordinary garden phloxes, but in its wild state, from New York to Georgia and westward, it is an erect plant 2–4 feet high, and has typically red-purple or even whitish flowers. It is of easy culture either in open woods or in usual garden soils.

For other species of phlox see the chapter devoted to plants of open, drier places.

SHORTIA. *Shortia galacifolia.* pH 5–6. A rare and beautiful wild flower, closely related to galax which is noted earlier in this chapter. It is practically stemless, bears small, ground-hugging, evergreen leaves which become bronzy in winter. The beautiful, bell-shaped, white or pinkish, solitary flowers are on slender stalks 6–8 inches high and are nodding. May-blooming. Unfortunately *Shortia* is not easily grown. It is better to start with purchased plants. Propagation of your own stock is difficult from seed and, in fact, most likely to fail. Division of the plant, about a month after flowering, is often successful if moisture and shade conditions are favorable. The most certain, but troublesome, method is to take cuttings in early summer, planted in a mixture of 1 part sand and 3 parts acid peat, in pots or pans. These should be put in a lath house or shaded cold-frame, kept moist, and by the following spring or the next one should be ready to plant out. It needs shade, moisture, and a mulch of oak leaves. Does well under rhododendrons. Shortia has an interesting history. It was first discovered by the French botanist Michaux early in the nineteenth century and completely lost until accidentally rediscovered by an herb collector in the mountains of North Carolina in 1878. Asa Gray visited the spot in May, 1879, and published an account of its rediscovery. Until recently it had no other name than Shortia, but the somewhat fanciful and wholly manufactured name of Oconee bells is used by some.

SNAKEROOT. *Cimicifuga racemosa,* often called bugbane or black snakeroot. A tall, rather coarse herb, often 3–6 feet high, with large, divided leaves and a spire-like cluster of small, white flowers, the clusters often branched and showy in June or July. It is of easy culture in dry or moist woods and is of value for bold effects, and because it blooms when most woodland plants are long past flowering. A related plant, *Cimicifuga americana,* is similar, but about half as high, and is native farther south so that it will stand more heat than the snakeroot.

SOLOMON'S-SEAL. *Polygonatum pubescens* (often listed as *Polygonatum biflorum*). An easily grown woodland herb common throughout the forested regions of eastern North America, except in the hot, dry woods of the coastal plain. It is 18–30 inches high and has alternate leaves, each with a pair, or few, bell-shaped, greenish-yellow flowers, which bloom in June or early July. Not very showy, but useful because of its ease of growth. It is readily propagated by division, when dormant, of its stout much-branched rootstock. A related, but coarser and taller species is *Polygonatum canaliculatum,* which must be collected from the wild or raised from seed, as dealers do not generally offer it. The plant is often 3½–5 feet high.

SPRING BEAUTY. *Claytonia virginica.* No wild flower withers so quickly as this little harbinger of spring. Its delicate small, pinkish-white flowers bloom in mid-April, the whole plant being scarcely 6 inches high. After flowering its equally delicate, narrow and slender leaves die down and the plant is dormant throughout the rest of the season and following winter. It can easily be dug from the wild, after flowers and leaves wither, and planted in almost any woods soil so long as it is damp or moist. In the wild the plant runs into swamps and even into sandy thickets so long as they are moist. A relative of it, *Claytonia caroliniana,* has broader leaves and grows in similar sites, only in cool mountain regions, and is not suited to the warm coastal plain. (See Color Plate 11.)

SPRING-BEAUTY

TOOTHWORT. *Dentaria diphylla.* pH 5–6. Also called crinkleroot and pepper-root. A May-flowering perennial with toothed rootstocks, a pair of 3-parted leaves, and small clusters of 4-petalled pinkish-white flowers in a loose cluster, the whole plant not usually over 8 inches high. It grows in rich, damp woods and should be planted in such sites, since it will not thrive in the open. The brittle rootstock is easily separable into pieces, each of which will make a new plant, if divided when dormant. A related plant, *Dentaria laciniata,* pH 6–7, has leaves with narrower segments and a jointed rootstock that is even more easily separable than in *Dentaria diphylla.*

TWINFLOWER. *Linnaea borealis.* pH 4–5. Well named *borealis,* for the twinflower grows, in some of its forms, throughout the subarctic regions, where it was discovered by Linnaeus and named for him. It somewhat resembles the partridgeberry noted earlier in this chapter, because it is a prostrate, evergreen vine, and its trailing stems send up a flower stalk, not over 4–5 inches high crowned with a pair of separate small, funnel-shaped, nodding, pinkish-white flowers, which bloom in June or July. It cannot be grown in warm, dry places, as it often inhabits cold bogs in Greenland and Alaska. It also thrives in mountain woods, often under evergreens, and so far as cultivation is concerned it must have deep shade, coolness, and moisture, as well as considerable acidity. (See Color Plate 16 (as *Linnaea americana*).)

TWISTED-STALK. *Streptopus roseus.* pH 5. A curious, lily-like herb with a zig-zag stalk 10–18 inches high. From each stalkless leaf there arises a small, stalked, rose-colored, bell-shaped flower, usually half hidden by the foliage; blooming in June. Not difficult to grow or propagate which may be done by dividing the often branched rootstock when the plant is dormant. It prefers reasonably moist, rich woods, preferably away from the coastal plain.

TRILLIUM OR WAKEROBIN. *Trillium.* These are among our most showy woodland wild flowers, often naturalized by wild gardeners, and, with proper conditions, not too difficult to grow. All of those below (there are many others) can be had from most dealers in woodland plants. It is strongly recommended that the amateur start with purchased plants, for raising trilliums from seed is a tricky and slow process. Trilliums, as the name suggests, have only three leaves, all grouped in a cluster, from which arises the single stalked or stalkless, often very showy flowers. These may be from ¾ to 1½ inches wide, and some of them are nodding; mostly May-flowering. The recommended woodland species are:

Nodding trillium. *Trillium cernuum.* pH 5–6. 8–15 inches high. Flowers, stalked, nodding, half hidden by the leaves, and white. (See Color Plate 28 (as Nodding Wake-robin).)

Purple trillium. *Trillium erectum.* pH 5–6. 8–15 inches high. Flowers stalked, erect, brownish-purple.

White trillium. *Trillium grandiflorum.* pH 6–7. 9–20 inches high, and the showiest of all the trilliums. Flowers stalked, erect, white nearly 2 inches wide.

Yellow trillium. *Trillium luteum.* pH 6–7. 9–18 inches. Flowers stalkless, yellow, not very showy, but the leaves handsomely mottled.

Toadshade. *Trillium sessile.* pH 6–7. 7–15 inches high. Flowers stalkless, brown-purple.

Painted trillium. *Trillium undulatum.* pH 4–5. 8–15 inches high. Flowers stalked, erect, white, streaked with purple, and the most showy trillium after *T. grandiflorum.*

Fortunately trilliums are not too difficult to grow if you have the right degree of acidity, as specified above, and a good, rich woods soil, either natural or made as described in the first chapter. The plants need a reasonable amount of moisture, good shade, and can be readily divided when dormant. They tend to spread if happy and left alone. If roots or bulblets are planted, plant them at least 4–6 inches deep. There is no finer wild garden vista than a shaded bank covered with the great white trillium.

Umbrella-leaf. *Diphylleia cymosa.* A curious, single-leaved plant before it is old enough to bloom, then bearing only two rather large, divided leaves. The plant is 1–2 feet high, its naked flower stalk bearing a small cluster of white flowers in May, followed by showy blue fruits on red stalks. The plant grows naturally only in the mountains from Virginia to Georgia and needs a cool, moist, shaded nook to do its best.

VIOLETS. *Viola.* Wild violets. As there are nearly 50 species of wild violets east of the Mississippi, no owner of a woodland garden will fail to dig some of them out. They are easily moved almost any time, and the only caution necessary is to put those in the shade that grow there, and to look out for the kinds that have their feet in wet places. The identification of the wild species is difficult, but one species is worth cultivating. It is the Confederate violet, *Viola priceana,* with the largest and showiest flowers of all violets. It does perfectly under shade or in full sunlight, self-seeds at a good rate, and in early May will make sheets of color in a few years. For another violet of dry, open places, see the chapter devoted to such plants.

VIRGINIA COWSLIP. *Mertensia virginica,* often called bluebell or lungwort. It is 10–18 inches high, with mostly basal leaves and a cluster of blue or pinkish flowers in a terminal cluster, which is one-sided and apt to curve at the tip. The plant is very showy, often cultivated in ordinary garden soils, but its home is rich, moist woods and it will do best in such places. May-flowering. As it is rather difficult to dig from the wild, the amateur will do best with purchased plants. (See Color Plate 23 (as Virginia Bluebells).)

WILD GERANIUM. *Geranium maculatum.* pH 5–6. These wild flowers have nothing to do with the garden geranium, which comes from South Africa and belongs to *Pelargonium.* The wild geranium of our woods is a perennial herb, 10–20 inches high, with divided leaves and a magenta-pink flower in a loose cluster, which blooms in May. It is easy to transfer from the woods and grows well in the wild garden, under deep or partial shade, or even in the open, so long as there is woods soil and reasonable moisture. (See Color Plate 9 (as Spotted Cranesbill).)

WILD GINGER. *Asarum canadense.* When the first settlers reached New England they found the Indians using the root of this plant to flavor food. Today it is grown in the woodland garden mostly because its handsome green leaves make an excellent groundcover in dense shade, which the plant prefers. Hidden by the leaves and scarcely protruding from the ground are the dark, reddish-brown flowers, which bloom in late April or May. There is no finer groundcover in shady places from May to October. It should have good, woodsy soil.

WINDFLOWER. *Anemonella thalictroides.* pH 5–6. Closely related to the anemones, noted earlier in this chapter, the windflower is much easier to grow. It is about 6–8 inches high with leaf-segments like a meadow rue, hence its other name of rue anemone. Flowers white, sometimes double, appearing in late April or early May. It is a plant of rich woods and should be planted in the woodland garden, as much out of the wind as possible. It has tiny tubers which can be easily moved after the plant dies down, in early June. It will completely disappear throughout the summer, but is one of our most certain signs of spring.

WOOD SORREL. *Oxalis acetosella.* pH 4–5. A delicate, trailing plant of high mountains and their cool, coniferous woods, not over 3–5 inches high, the 3-parted, notched leaves suggesting the shamrock. Flower solitary at the end of a thread-thick stalk, generally white but veined with handsome pink stripes, usually June-blooming, but often later. Its culture should only be attempted in cool, moist sites where there is deep humus and plenty of shade. In the Adirondacks it makes unforgettable pictures of loveliness under the shade of spruces and firs.

For all native orchids see the chapter devoted to them and for a few of our most difficult of woodland plants see the last chapter.)

For Thickets and Open Places

CHAPTER III

NOT ALL of us have natural woodlands or can make them to conform to the relatively exacting requirements outlined in the first two chapters. But this need not stop anyone from having a garden of native plants, some of them very beautiful, none of which need dense shade or rich humus, and some of which thrive only because there is neither. Some others, also, do well without the constant moisture that so many woodland plants demand.

In walking along any country lane, or even some modern highways, there are hundreds of wild flowers that thrive, either in full sun or in the partial shade of small shrubs, or perhaps under an occasional tree. Such places breed thickets, which are so common as scarcely to need definition. But many of us have natural thickets whether we like them or not. Technically their chief characteristic is the absence of trees (there may be small saplings) and a thick or sparse growth of shrubs or tall weeds. There is little or no humus, except that which is inherent in all good topsoil, more or less constant exposure to either full sunshine, or the fitful shade of open shrubs, no protection from wind, and periods of natural drought.

Plants which thrive in such places are a boon to the wild gardener. Not all of them are easy to transplant, but most of them are far easier to establish than any of the plants mentioned in the second chapter. To those with weedy and maybe unsightly thickets, with often nondescript vegetation; to others with dry banks or open places that are neither garden nor lawn, the plants in the list below will be the answer to the often troublesome question, "What can I do with such a place?"

The plants in the list are suited to such sites, but not if the place is moist or wet. If it is shrubby and wet, it is on the way to becoming a swamp. If wet and open, it may be a bog, marsh, or meadow. All these terms are defined, and the plants for each will be found in Chapter V. Also, if your dry or open place is nearly pure sand, the plants for it should be sought in Chapter IV.

The soils in which plants for thickets and open places grow naturally are as varied as our landscape. Most of them tolerate a variety of soil types, and those that demand special mixtures are noted. No plants are included here that are especially difficult, these being reserved for the last chapter even if they grow in the open such as the incomparable bearberry and the elusive *Loiseleuria*. No orchids are included, as these are all treated in Chapter VI.

In the native flora there are hundreds of species that naturally grow in open places or thickets, but many of them are too wild for taming and most of them have flowers too inconspicuous to be worth a place in any wild garden. Also most of them are not in the lists of dealers in native plants so that, without a lot of trial and error, their adaptability to culture in the garden is unknown. Some enthusiasts say that *any* wild flower can be grown in the garden, but for practical purposes, and for busy people who do not want too many failures, it is better to stick to those that have been tried and not found wanting.

All the genera below, except one or two, are available from dealers in native plants, and some are in the catalogs of all good nurseries. They can also be raised from seed, but these are generally not in the seedsmen's catalogs and hence must be collected. All are perennials and should be treated as you do ordinary garden perennials from seed.

If your thicket has a miscellaneous variety of weedy plants, which is the usual condition, you cannot expect most of the plants in the following list to compete with them without some help. Clear out (by digging) unwanted weedy growth, making little or large patches or embayments among the shrubs in which to naturalize the plants of your choice. Some are so sturdy that they can fight their own battles, like the asters, goldenrods, coneflower, ox-eye, black Sampson, etc. But others, especially the first year or two, will need protection from too dominant weeds, particularly if your favorites are low and the weeds coarse and high.

Most of the plants in the list have a considerable tolerance for soils with normal acidity and alkalinity, within the range of pH 6–7. A few demand more acid conditions, and a handful appear to favor limestone regions and hence more alkaline sites. All such are noted, and those without a pH value can safely be grown in any ordinary garden soil or in sites where weedy thickets thrive.

If acidity must be provided for, beyond that of the natural site, peat or sphagnum moss may be mixed with the native soil, or you can add aluminum sulfate to it. (See Chapter I for details.) You will not, in your thicket, be adding peat or sphagnum to increase the moisture-holding capacity of the soil, although this will do no harm, but only to control its acidity.

If, on the other hand, lime is indicated, use it sparingly to bring the soil up to the required degree of alkalinity. (See Chapter I for details.) Beyond the usual watering of newly planted material, most of these plants should thrive with normal rainfall, unless you live in a region of semi-desert conditions. And if your soil has much gravel and sand, even if there is normal rainfall, there may be occasional local droughts, in which case you may have to water. Some of the species grow on dry prairies and will consequently stand any deficiency of rainfall that is likely in usual garden areas.

PLANTS FOR THICKETS AND OPEN PLACES

ADAM'S-NEEDLE. *Yucca filamentosa.* A stout, coarse perennial, with a rosette of basal, long, sword-shaped leaves that are spiny at the tip. From the center of the leaves there springs a flower stalk from 3–7 feet high crowded towards the summit with a dense cluster of white, waxy flowers. It is a close relative of the fantastic joshua trees of the Mohave Desert, admirably suited to the dry soils of the coastal plain, and blooms in early summer. Its cultivation is easy.

ASTER. *Aster.* A genus comprising over 60 species in eastern North America where they make up most of the autumnal color except for the goldenrods. No wild aster is yellow, and some of our white, blue, red, and lavender species have, mostly in England, produced the hybrid Michaelmas daisies, none of which is wild in America. Of the 60 species the following will be found most useful for thickets and open places. All, except *Aster spectabilis,* are of very easy culture, and if dug from the wild, preferably after flowering, can readily be grown. Some of them if watered occasionally and given a little fertilizer or manure will approach the Michaelmas daisies in profusion of bloom and color.

Aster cordifolius. 24–40 inches high, with large basal, heart-shaped leaves and the blue or purple flower heads nearly one inch wide, in an open, branched cluster.

Aster ericoides. 15–30 inches high, with hundreds of tiny narrow leaves scarcely one inch long. Flower heads white, scarcely 1/3 inch wide, but produced in such profusion in a complex, branching cluster, that the plant is a mass of bloom.

Aster laevis. 15–25 inches high, the leaves often stem-clasping, but not heart-shaped. Flower heads about 1½ inches wide, blue or pinkish-purple, in a somewhat sparsely flowered, open cluster.

Aster lateriflorus. 20–35 inches high, the stems usually several, with roughish, willow-like leaves. Flower heads about ½ inch wide, generally white, but occasionally pinkish-tinged, in a much-branched cluster.

Aster linariifolius. Not over 16–18 inches high, often less, with tough wiry stems, and rough narrow leaves that are scarcely ¼ inch wide and about 1½ inches long. Flower heads solitary or in a sparse cluster, but showy, nearly 1½ inches wide, violet. Difficult to kill in the most open, sandy or rocky places.

Aster patens. 8–20 inches high, the broadish but pointed leaves roughish and stem-clasping. Flower heads few, often solitary, or in a sparsely branched cluster, but nearly 1½ inches wide and blue, hence showy.

Aster spectabilis. pH 5–6. 12–36 inches high, the leaves mostly basal, slender and without marginal teeth. Flower heads nearly 1¾ inches wide, very showy, the rays deep violet-purple. One of the most spectacular of our native asters. It grows in open sandy woods, mostly under pines, and needs such a soil, although it will grow in the open. Do not plant it in stony soil or where there is heavy clay.

The New England and New York Asters, among our finest wild asters, prefer more moisture and will be found in Chapter V.

Blazing Star. *Liatris.* This group of mostly prairie herbs is a boon to those with hot dry banks, poor soil, and little water. They are wand-like plants, mostly 12–30 inches high, and have showy, button-like heads of flowers. All are of the easiest culture. Many species are known, but the following will suffice for most growers. All are pinkish-purple, and bloom in late summer.

Liatris graminifolia. 10–30 inches high, the flower heads about ½ inch wide.

Liatris pycnostachya. 20–36 inches high, the flower heads about ¾ inches wide, crowded in close, wand-like clusters.

Liatris scariosa. 12–30 inches high, the flower heads stalked, about ¾ inches wide, more or less distant from one another.

Butterfly-weed. *Asclepias tuberosa.* A dry-soil herb, often called pleurisy-root, and perhaps the most showy of all the native milkweeds. It is inclined to sprawl, is never more than 15–20 inches high and has gorgeous orange flowers in close, head-like clusters. It is perfectly at home on the hot, dry, coastal plain, prefers rather sandy soil, but is hard to get established. It has a deep root (1–3 feet) and all of it must be dug (when the plant is dormant); as the roots are brittle considerable care is needed. Plant it in a mixture of half sand and half soil—no clay or rocks. (See Color Plate 15.) For the swamp milkweed see Chapter V.

Bluebell. *Campanula rotundifolia.* 4–12 inches, and a weak-stemmed perennial with narrow stem leaves and a few, small, heart-shaped basal ones that soon wither. Flower small, bell-shaped, and brilliantly blue. The bluebell is not for the coastal plain, as it grows in rocky clefts in the mountains, and even on beaches up to Labrador. Suitable only for cool, open, preferably rocky places.

Blue-eyed Grass. *Sisyrinchium angustifolium.* A grass-like herb, 4–12 inches high, the slender leaves over-topped by the sparse cluster of vividly bluish-violet flowers, which are about ¾ inch wide. Of easy culture in a variety of open places, even if they are wet, but generally found in dry fields.

Catchfly. *Silene.* Sticky herbs with generally showy flowers. Of the many North American kinds, two are particularly suited to open places.

Wild pink. *Silene caroliniana.* pH 7–8. A slender, tufted perennial, 3–8 inches hgih with a deep taproot which must be dug out (when plant is dormant). Flowers few, in a close cluster, pink or whitish pink, the five petals blunt. Not too easy to transplant, but suitable for dry, rocky places. May-blooming. Its roots are brittle and need care in handling.

Fire pink. *Silene virginica.* pH 5–6. Not usually over 8–12 inches high. Flowers bright crimson, very showy, the petals notched. Easier to grow than the wild pink, but most at home on rocky ledges or in dry, reasonably sandy places. (See Color Plate 7 (as Firepink).)

Cinquefoil. *Potentilla tridentata.* pH 5. A low, woody-

Russell Tinling Pansie

SWAMP ROSEMALLOW
Hibiscus moscheutos

Harold D. Roberts

PURPLE POPPY-MALLOW
Callirhoë involucrata

Harold D. Roberts

SNOW-ON-THE-MOUNTAIN
Lepadena marginata

Wild Flower Preservation Society

COMMON SPRINGBEAUTY
Claytonia virginica

PLATE 12

Harold D. Roberts

SULPHURFLOWER
Eriogonum umbellatum

Russell Tinling Pansie

LARGE-FLOWERED SENSITIVE-PEA
Chamaecrista fasciculata

Joseph R. Swain

BUNCHBERRY
Chamaepericlymenum canadense (*Cornus canadensis*)

PLATE 13

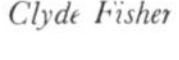

Clyde Fisher

LEAVENWORTH'S ERYNGO
Eryngium leavenworthii

Harold D. Roberts

PURPLE PRAIRIECLOVER
Petalostemon purpureum

Walter Henricks Hodge

TRAILING-ARBUTUS
Epigaea repens

Walter Henricks Hodge

COMMON BLUETS
Houstonia caerulea

Clyde Fisher

YELLOW JESSAMINE
Gelsemium sempervirens

stemmed perennial, mostly on rocky mountain summits from Greenland to the mountains of Georgia, not well suited to the coastal plain. It grows 4–9 inches high and has a few-flowered cluster of white flowers. Best suited to rocky places in the north, and if you have no rocks it needs a soil of rock screenings, sand, and enough peat to bring the mixture to pH 5.

CINQUEFOIL

CONEFLOWER. *Rudbeckia triloba.* 20–50 inches high and a rather coarse, stout perennial, the large leaves 3-lobed; flower heads yellow or orange, at least 2½ inches wide, arranged in a lax cluster, rather showy and summer blooming. It is not particular as to soil, and in some of its wild forms even grows in moist places. A relative is *Rudbeckia laciniata,* which may be 7–9 feet high, has much cut leaves, and yellow flower heads at least 3–4 inches wide. From it was derived the common goldenglow of the gardens. No one should ever grow the black-eyed Susan, *Rudbeckia hirta,* in spite of its showy flowers, because this predominately prairie plant has become one of the most pestiferous weeds in the east; very difficult to eradicate.

EUPATORIUM. *Eupatorium.* Tall, handsome, sometimes a little weedy herbs, with showy heads of flowers mostly blooming in midsummer, comprising a score of different kinds of which the mist-flower and boneset are plants of moist or wet places and are listed in Chapter V. Of the species found mostly in dry open places those most worthy of cultivation are:

Eupatorium hyssopifolium, 10–25 inches high, with groups of 4 narrow, ashy-gray leaves. Flower heads small, misty, white, in dense, rather showy clusters. One of the best plants for dry open places in our native flora, particularly suited to sandy soils along the coastal plain. September-blooming.

White snakeroot. *Eupatorium rugosum.* 15–30 inches high, the relatively broad leaves opposite. Flower heads small, white in an almost flat-topped cluster, blooming in August. Good for filtered shade under shrubs, even sometimes growing under trees, but also at home in the open.

Joe-Pye weed. *Eupatorium purpureum.* 3–5 feet high, the long, ovalish leaves in groups of 3 or 4. Flower heads very small, but hundreds of them crowded into a convex cluster, mostly pinkish-purple, the plant hence very showy in August. Typically at home in dry thickets and of the easiest culture. Close relatives grow in moister places (see Chapter V).

FIREWEED. *Epilobium angustifolium.* pH 5–6. Often called great willow-herb, and from 3–5 feet high, it invariably follows forest fires, spreads into thickets, and often covers large areas with its purple or pinkish-white bloom in midsummer. Leaves willow-like. Flowers in a long, wand-like, loose cluster, quite showy. It will not be too easy to establish, and the easiest way is to collect its copious seed and sow them in a mixture of half sand and half acid peat. Some strains of it live in rich woods humus.

FLOWERING SPURGE. *Euphorbia corollata.* 1–3 feet high, the oblongish leaves with a milky juice. Flowers small, very numerous, in an open, much-branched cluster that may be 4–9 inches wide and showy in midsummer. It has a deep root and care must be used in digging it out, preferably when the plant is dormant. Fine for open grassy places, banks, etc.

GAILLARDIA. *Gaillardia aristata.* 10–25 inches high. Not so showy as the generally annual, garden gaillardias, this inhabitant of our western plains, sometimes called blanket-flower, is perennial and has yellow flower heads, 3–4 inches wide with a rose-purple center, hence very showy. It will grow almost anywhere in the open, including the ordinary garden, and blooms all summer.

GOLDENROD. *Solidago.* An immense group of often rather weedy herbs, a few of them showy because of the numerous yellow flower heads often in striking clusters. They present no difficulties in growing, and some species threaten to become a nuisance, so rampant is their growth, and so easily do they spread. Nearly all are tall herbs, with fibrous, easily dug roots; of over 60 kinds known in the eastern states (some think there are 75 species) the two below are the only ones included here. Blooming in late summer and early fall.

Solidago canadensis. 20–40 inches high, the innumerable yellow, tiny flower heads in a large terminal cluster, each branch of which has flower heads only on one side of it and arched. This is nearly our most common goldenrod and of the easiest culture. (See Color Plate 17.)

Solidago odora. 15–30 inches high, the narrow leaves beautifully anise-scented when crushed, or there may be a scentless strain in some plants. Flowers in a terminal, arching, one-sided cluster, odorless. It can be grown in any open place and its chief attraction is the aromatic, crushed foliage.

GROUND PINK. *Phlox subulata.* Prostrate and forming dense mats. Few of our native plants have become such general garden favorites as the moss pink or rock pink which are other common names for *Phlox subulata.* Its leaves are very short, needle-like and numerous, and from the mat of foliage spring many close clusters of typically magenta or pink flowers (often white in a horticultural variety), mostly in late April or early May. It grows naturally in open places, either sandy or rocky and should be grown in full sunshine. It is one of the most satisfactory of spring groundcovers. A related species, *Phlox amoena,* is taller, not quite so dense in growth, and its flowers are reddish-purple, mostly May-blooming. It will stand some shade.

HORSE BALM. *Collinsonia canadensis.* A branching perennial, 18–30 inches high, with broadish, opposite leaves, and an open, lax cluster of yellow, 2-lipped, irregular flowers that are about ¾ inch long. It grows in open woods or along the edges of them and is best grown in thickets where it gets partial shade for at least part of the day. Its August bloom is welcome as most spring wild flowers are either dormant or long finished blooming. The plant is sometimes called citronella, from the odor of its crushed foliage, although it has nothing to do with true citronella, which is a tropical grass.

INDIAN PHYSIC. *Gillenia trifoliata.* A spirea-like perennial herb 15–36 inches high, often called Bowman's-root, once thought to have medicinal value. It has compound, sharply toothed leaves and open, rather lax clusters of May-blooming white, not very showy flowers. Of the easiest culture in any open place, preferably away from the coastal plain as its natural habitat is in thin upland woods or clearings in them, mostly in the mountains.

LILY-OF-THE-VALLEY. *Convallaria majalis.* So well known to most gardeners as scarcely to need any note here. The experts differ as to its true home, but besides its occurrence as a wild plant in Europe and Asia, it certainly seems wild in the mountains from Virginia to the Great Smokies. Whatever its true source it is common in many ordinary gardens, in shade, full sun, and in partial shade. Purchased plants put in ordinary garden soil, preferably with plenty of humus, soon spread, and its May-blooming, white, fragrant flowers are a delight in any garden. It does better in sites that are not too dry.

LUPINE. *Lupinus perennis.* pH 5–6. This beautiful, native, blue-flowered lupine which thrives so well in open, sandy places in the eastern states presents a challenge to all wild gardeners. It is not offered by any ordinary nurseryman, nor do seedsmen carry it, so you must get it from the wild to have it at all. The plant is 8–15 inches high, and in May its clusters of blue, pea-like flowers are profuse. It is quite useless to attempt digging it out until thoroughly dormant (in other words, apparently dead). Get *all* the roots and with as much soil as possible. Plant them deeply in a mixture of sand and soil, mulch them with pine needles, and water them only with rainwater when first set out. If you collect seed in June or July, plant it at once in flats or pans filled with an acid mixture of two parts sand, one part shopped sphagnum moss, and one part loam. The seeds should be niched with a file and soaked in warm water overnight, before planting. They will not germinate until the next spring and need constant attention as to watering, for they must not dry out. Lupine is definitely not for the impatient, but is one of our loveliest flowers for dry, open, and sandy places, preferably on the coastal plain.

Monkshood. *Aconitum uncinatum.* A weak, sprawling perennial, often 30–40 inches high, often clambering over other plants. Its deeply cut leaves and showy, helmet-shaped blue flowers make it an attractive plant for the partial shade of thickets, or even in open woods, mostly in the mountains. Both it and the related *Aconitum reclinatum,* which is lower and less vine-like, are best started as purchased plants, and neither presents any particular difficulty. Both are summer-blooming.

Oswego Tea. *Monarda didyma.* A very showy, scarlet-flowered herb, 15–25 inches high, with opposite leaves that are most aromatic. Flowers irregular, nearly 2 inches long, crowded in a dense, head-like, terminal cluster, mostly in August. It is quite adaptable, easy to grow, and is found naturally in or at the edge of woods, in thickets, and in the open. An ashy-foliaged relative, *Monarda fistulosa,* with less conspicuous, lavender flowers is best used only in dry thickets or open prairies. (See Color Plate 25.)

Ox-eye. *Heliopsis helianthoides.* A coarse, sunflower-like perennial herb 3–5 feet high, with an often rough stem, opposite, toothed leaves and a yellow flower head that may be 4–5 inches wide, in a sparse cluster. It is easy to grow and perhaps not worth it, except for those who have thicket-like places, fence-corners, waste places, etc. where its August bloom may be welcome. It is next to impossible to kill it and it may spread to be a nuisance.

Pasque-flower. *Anemone patens.* A beautiful silky-hairy herb native on prairies and not at all like the woodland anemones mentioned in Chapter II. It is a perennial herb 4–10 inches high, with much divided, mostly basal leaves, and a stiff stalk crowned with a usually solitary, blue or purplish flower, 2½ inches wide, that blooms in April, before the leaves expand. The flower is followed by a plumy, silky fruit. It grows up to the Arctic Circle and should not be tried in hot, dry

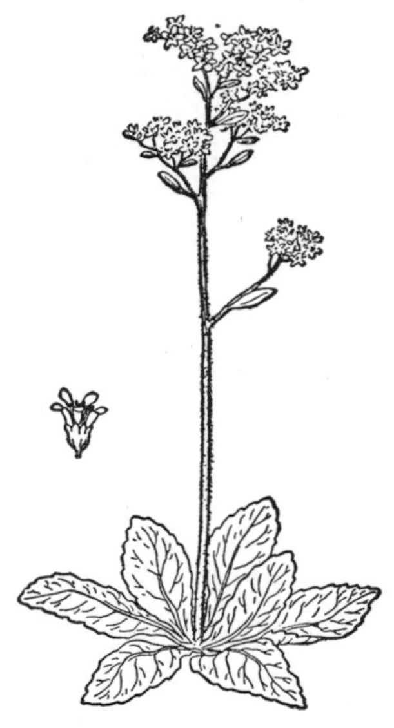

EARLY SAXIFRAGE

places along the coastal plain. Division of its roots in late fall is an easy method of propagation. It needs full sun. (See Color Plate I (as *Pulsatilla*).)

PURPLE CONEFLOWER. *Echinacea purpurea.* Closely related to the common coneflower, treated earlier in this chapter, but with the flower heads reddish-purple instead of yellow, the head frequently 2½–3 inches wide, its petal-like rays tending to droop. The plant is stout, rather bold and coarse, 3–5 feet high and next to impossible to kill, even in a prolonged drought. Easily divided in fall or spring, and a useful plant for almost impossible places. Summer-blooming, the flowers sometimes lasting a month. It is also known as black Sampson. (See Color Plate 21.)

EARLY SAXIFRAGE. *Saxifraga virginiensis.* Often called rock saxifrage from its inhabiting rocky cliffs or ledges. It mostly grows in the open and is one of our earliest wild flowers to bloom, often by mid-April. It is scarcely 4–6 inches high, with chiefly basal leaves, and a branching flower cluster, the small petals white. Not difficult to dig from the wild, but it should be grown only in rocky places, preferably not on the coastal plain.

SHOOTING-STAR. *Dodecatheon Meadia.* A beautiful perennial, 5–10 inches high, with a basal rosette of leaves and an erect flower stalk crowned with pinkish-white or lavender flowers, the petals of which are turned downward, and the erect center of the flower (the stamens) standing above the petals. The nearly cyclamen-like flower blooms in late May or early June. Not difficult to grow in the shade of thickets, in rocky places, or even in the woods, but not advised for the dry, sandy soils of the coastal plain.

SPIKENARD. *Aralia racemosa.* A handsome perennial, 3–6 feet high, its huge leaves much parted and divided, and suggesting some of its tropical relatives. Flower cluster much-branched, the individual flowers small, greenish-white, not very showy, but the whole cluster quite striking. Often growing in rich woods, it often invades clearings in the forest and can be planted under thickets, preferably in the upland or mountainous part of our area. Do not dig it up except in the late fall or early spring. Summer-blooming.

STAR-GRASS. *Hypoxis hirsuta.* pH 5–6. A grass-like plant with small, yellow, star-like flowers, the whole plant scarcely

8–10 inches tall, usually less. In nature often associated with blue-eyed grass, already noted earlier in this chapter. It is common in and along the edges of the thin woods of the coastal plain and admirably suited to sandy soil of such places. It blooms in May–June, but is not very showy. It makes a splendid color contrast with the blue-eyed grass.

STONECROP. *Sedum.* Scarcely any rock garden is furnished without several species of stonecrops most of which are at home in rocky open places. Of the 15 wild species found within our range two are useful for open and even for fairly dry places in the wild garden. They are fairly closely related to the common houseleek of the garden and are of easy culture. They are:

Sedum telephioides. Perhaps only a native American form of the orpine (*Sedum telephium*) which is common in gardens. Our plant is 4–10 inches high, with thick, fleshy leaves and a terminal, fairly close cluster of small, pinkish flowers in September. It is better suited to open rocky places in the mountains than to the coastal plain.

Sedum ternatum. A low, creeping plant with small, fleshy leaves in clusters of three or less. From this arises a lax flower stalk, not usually over 6 inches high, crowned by a sprawling, loose cluster of small, white flowers in May or June. Particularly good as a groundcover on rock ledges, but preferably in the mountains.

SUNDROPS. *Oenothera fruticosa.* A relative of the evening primrose, but day-blooming and with handsome yellow flowers, about 1 inch wide, in an open, sparse cluster, June-blooming. The plant is about 20 inches high and is at home in dry, sandy places or in fields. Its culture presents no difficulties. There are many relatives, but *Oenothera fruticosa* is one of the best.

SUNFLOWER. *Helianthus.* Tall, rather weedy, often very striking relatives of the huge annual sunflower of the gardens. Both of those below are perennials, chosen from nearly 20 native sorts because they are suited to open thickets, and to most other places so long as they are not shady. They are coarse plants, like the coneflower, the purple coneflower, and the ox-eye, to which they are related. Like them they are of the easiest culture, can be readily divided, but care must be used to prevent their becoming a nuisance, as they are rather rampant. All bear yellow flowers in midsummer.

Helianthus mollis. 20–40 inches high, the stem and leaves densely hairy. Flower heads daisy-like, rich golden yellow, not numerous, about 2½ inches wide. Does well in sandy places.

Helianthus salicifolius. Tall, smooth-stemmed perennial, often 8–9 feet high, with long, slender, willow-like leaves. Flower heads nearly 3 inches wide, clear yellow. This sunflower grows naturally in limestone regions and is best grown in pH 7–8.

TICKSEED. *Coreopsis.* Useful garden plants because their showy flowers last well after picking. Of the many species found in North America, only three are especially chosen for open, dry places. All are yellow-flowered, except *Coreopsis rosea* which will be found in Chapter V, as it grows in wet places. Much the commonest species is the first one, as it is in many gardens, and often "escapes" into fields and roadsides. All are of the simplest possible culture and can be divided almost any time.

Coreopsis lanceolata. 8–20 inches high. Flower head nearly 2 inches wide, numerous and showy. Good for thickets, sandy places or fields.

Coreopsis tripteris. 30–50 inches high. Flower heads about

1¾ inches wide, not so numerous as in the one above. It will grow almost anywhere.

Coreopsis verticillata. A somewhat weak-stemmed perennial, 12–20 inches high, the leaves narrow, almost thread-like. Flower heads relatively few, about 1 inch wide. Best suited to the dry, almost sandy soils along the coastal plain.

VIOLET. *Viola.* For most kinds of violet see the woodland species in Chapter II. But the bird's-foot violet, *Viola pedata,* pH 6, is not only one of the most showy of all native violets, but about the only one that thrives in open, dry places, either in sand or on rocky ledges with little soil. The almost pansy-like flower has two upper petals that are dark violet, while the three lower ones are purple-lilac, May-blooming. It needs a sandy or gritty soil, full sunshine, and can be dug from the wild after the flowering period. Not too easy to establish. (See Color Plate 5.)

WILD INDIGO. *Baptisia australis.* A stiff perennial often 3–4 feet high, with compound leaves and showy terminal, finger-like clusters of handsome, blue, pea-like flowers, blooming in May or June. It is at home in gravelly or sandy places, and it is best to start with purchased plants. A relative, *Baptisia tinctoria,* often called false indigo, has fewer, smaller and yellow flowers. Its chief virtue is its ability to grow in the hot, dry, sandy soils of the coastal plain.

Sands and the Seashore

CHAPTER IV

THE PECULIAR conditions that obtain in any area occupied by pure sand are so unfavorable that most gardeners are likely to abandon the idea of growing anything. The site, it must be admitted, is about as bad as anything could be, so severe that all ordinary garden plants will perish. But that does not mean that nothing will grow in pure sand.

How unfavorable open sand can be is well illustrated by the ecological conditions that are common there. In the first place there is complete exposure to the bitter winds of winter, with no protective screen of shrubs or trees, no shade, and a soil that, at least at the surface, has practically no capacity for holding moisture. On any bright, sunny day try putting the bulb of a thermometer only an inch deep in the sand about mid-day. It will read anywhere from 110° to 140° F, and in some really warm regions (Arizona and New Mexico) it may be 10–15° above this. If, moreover, you consider the hot, drying winds in such places, it all adds up to a pretty dreary prospect as the site for any sort of a garden.

But nature and the plants that grow naturally in sand seem to realize that, if conditions are tough, there are things that can be done, and have been done, about it to overcome the blazing heat, lack of surface moisture, drying winds, and other unfavorable factors. From a study of the wild plants that are practically confined to such places we learn two important lessons for the sand gardener.

All plants maintain a proper balance between water intake and water loss even if growing in pure sand. When that balance fails there is first wilting, and if it goes on too long death is inevitable. How they keep their balance is instructive. In the first place most of them have deep root systems, far below the heat of the surface. Here they find the necessary moisture, which in many of them may not be too much because of the action of a mechanism that, if not consciously intelligent, has all the advantages of it.

Normal water loss from plants, which must go on to keep them in full health, all comes from water vapor transpired (not evaporated) from microscopic pores that are mostly on the under side of leaves, known collectively as stomata. There is an elaborate mechanism for opening wide these pores or almost completely closing them over periods of emergency. This is peculiarly effective in plants of the desert and in what we call sand plants.

But nature does not stop with the mere opening and closing of stomata. Many sand plants have reduced leaf areas, or no leaves at all like our prickly pear, and even if there is an expanded leaf blade it is often covered by dense hairs, or is ashy gray, or in some species it appears as if varnished. All of these, and many other hidden contrivances, are effective devices to retard transpiration. They help the plant to keep a proper water balance and incidentally contribute one of the greatest factors of safety in the cultivation of all sand plants.

With nature granting us this boon, how can we cooperate with her in the attempt to grow these hardy inhabitants of our most unfavorable environment? As was noted earlier, most sand plants have deep roots, and some have them thickened, probably for water storage. To ensure success *we must dig out all these roots,* and only when the plant is dormant. Some of those roots reach down to layers where there is comparatively cool moisture.

It may be that when the plant becomes dormant it has all but disappeared, at least for that season, in which case you scarcely know where to dig. The only remedy is to put a stake down while the plant is growing to mark the site of future digging. Once the root is dug out, without breaking it (nor must it ever be "torn up by the roots"), keep the root moist in wet bagging or paper and plant it as quickly as possible.

In planting these denizens of the sand, see that the hole is ample, freshly dug so that it does not dry out, and that your specimen is put at its old level in the sand, or even a little deeper. It invites certain failure to plant such specimens in the upper, hot layers of the sand, for next summer's heat will certainly doom them.

Another factor apparently inherent in all sands and the plants that grow in them is aeration. Not much technically is known of the effect of air spaces in sand, nor of the part it plays in the ecology of desert or sand plants. But experience has shown that such plants do not thrive if the soil is compacted. For the sand gardener this may be the factor between success or failure. If the site into which you plant your specimen has any underlying layers of ordinary soil, especially if this has any clay or silt in it, remove it. Never firm the plant in by tamping the sand—keep the air spaces free. If you put your plant in during dormancy there is no need to water it, and rainfall should take care of it subsequently.

These general principles of the ecology of all sand plants have been elaborated perhaps beyond your patience, but they are essential and apply to all the plants in this chapter. Failure to observe them merely invites your own failure. By following them, or modifying them as directed for certain species which are noted at the proper place, you will be working with nature in what is admittedly one of the hardest kinds of gardening.

There is one other factor, which splits this chapter in two, and that is salt. Along the seashore and in the dunes behind them, the sand is always impregnated with more or less salt, driven in by salt spray, sea fogs, etc. The plants that grow in such places will not generally grow in pure sand, and most ordinary sand plants will not tolerate much if any salt. In other words, the sand plants and seashore plants are in separate lists.

As to the availability of the plants in both the lists, it is generally nil. Almost no nursery has any of them, and you will thus have to collect your own. Presumably if you need to have a sand or seaside garden, you live near such sites, and the collection of material will not be too difficult. Whenever the plant is offered by dealers, it will be noted.

SAND PLANTS

There are not many native plants that will thrive in pure sand and, as previously outlined, care must be used in getting them established. A few of the plants in Chapter III are so much at home in sandy places that they should not be ignored.

Those from the chapter entitled "For Thickets and Open Places" that may safely be tried also in pure sand are the following. Because descriptions of them have been given in Chapter III, they need not be repeated here:

Adam's needle. *Yucca filamentosa.*
Bird's-foot violet. *Viola pedata.*
Eupatorium hyssopifolium.
Flowering spurge. *Euphorbia corollata.*
Wild indigo. *Baptisia australis.*

There is, of course, one of the finest of our sand plants, the bearberry (*Arctostaphylos uva-ursi*), useful for covering sandy banks, and one of the best groundcovers among our native plants. But its culture and digging from the wild present sufficient difficulty so that it will be found in the last chapter, which is confined to admittedly tough assignments.

Quite a few of the plants in the list call for a pH considerably more acid than that of pure sand. For such plants it will be necessary to add chopped-up sphagnum or shredded peat moss to bring the site to the desired acidity. For the details of this see Chapter I.

The rather meagre list of native sand plants follows:

AARON'S ROD. *Thermopsis caroliniana.* 3–4 feet high, the foliage ashy-gray. Flowers pea-like, golden yellow, in a long spire-like terminal cluster and hence far more showy than most sand plants. Not easy to dig up as the roots are deep. Propagation is best assured by sowing fresh seed, which is plentiful. Put the seeds about ¼ inches deep in a mixture of half sand and half shredded sphagnum moss. With proper care and watering they should germinate the following spring and can be put in the permanent site that autumn. Dealers also carry living plants.

PLATE 15

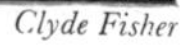

Clyde Fisher

BUTTERFLYWEED
Asclepias tuberosa

Joseph R. Swain

ORANGE HAWKWEED
Hieracium aurantiacum

PLATE 16

Helen Cruickshank

TWINFLOWER
Linnaea americana

Hugo H. Schroder

MAYPOP
Passiflora incarnata

Joseph R. Swain

COMMON CHICORY
Cichorium intybus

PLATE 17

Lawrence D. Hiett

NEW ENGLAND ASTER
Aster novae-angliae

Harold D. Roberts

SHORT-PODDED PRIMROSE
Lavauxia brachycarpa

Clyde Fisher

CANADA GOLDENROD
Solidago canadensis

Wild Flower Preservation Society

BLACK-EYED-SUSAN
Rudbeckia serotina

Clyde Fisher

EASTERN FRINGED GENTIAN
Anthopogon crinitum (Gentiana crinita)

Walter Henricks Hodge

LARGE MARSH-PINK
Sabbatia dodecandra

Broom Crowberry. *Corema conradi.* pH 4–5. This is much safer to start from purchased plants, although only dealers in native material are likely to have it. The plant is actually a low, woody shrub, not usually over 8 inches high, but forming dense mats that may be 3–5 feet in diameter. The

COLIC-ROOT

leaves are minute, heath-like, and scarcely ¼ inch long. Flowers small, crowded in a dense, head-like cluster, and showy in late April and May. It is one of our rarest native plants, but thrives in the hot, sandy, pine barrens of New Jersey, and in a few other scattered localities.

Colic-root. *Aletris farinosa.* pH 5. The adaptability of the colic-root, or unicorn-root as it is also called, is so great that it will grow in hot, dry sand and also in moist, or even wet, sandy barrens. Almost no dealers carry it so that it must be dug up from the wild. It has a basal rosette of stiffish, narrow leaves, from which springs a spire-like cluster of small, white, lily-like flowers, blooming in June or July. The plant is usually less than 15 inches high and may be found from New England to Florida in sand, and west of the mountains in dry prairies to Minnesota and eastern Texas.

FROSTWEED. *Helianthemum canadense.* While cultivated frostweeds are numerous, they are usually plants for ordinary garden soils. This native species is a sand-tolerant perennial with rather glistening, hairy foliage and few or solitary yellow flowers, mostly in June or July, that are often about 1–1½ inches wide. The frostweed, which is not over 12 inches high, must be collected from the sandy places from Maine to North Carolina and westward. Its culture is no more difficult than other sand plants.

GOLDEN ASTER. *Chrysopsis falcata.* A glistening-white, densely hairy, tufted perennial, not usually over 8 inches high, growing naturally in hot sands from New England to New Jersey. It is of easy culture and can be dug up from the wild, as few dealers carry it. The yellow, daisy-like flowers bloom in midsummer. A larger-flowered relative, *Chrysopsis mariana,* is not quite so hairy and inhabits not only sandy places, but thin pine woods and even fields. It blooms in August or early September.

PRICKLY PEAR. *Opuntia compressa.* This is the only cactus that grows naturally east of the Allegheny Mountains, although its relatives in the deserts of our southwest are very numerous. The plant has no permanent leaves, but flat, leaf-like joints covered with prickles and a few spines. It is nowhere common, but is carried by dealers in native cacti. The whole plant, with its swollen, leaf-like joints, is not over 8–10 inches high, generally prostrate, and forming prickly mats when mature. Its showy yellow flowers, nearly 4 inches wide, bloom in midsummer. It may be in some catalogs under its old name of *Opuntia vulgaris.*

SAND MYRTLE. *Leiophyllum buxifolium.* pH 4–5. A pine-barren, low evergreen shrub, not over 8–10 inches high, usually less, with small, box-like leaves and a terminal, head-like cluster of tiny white or pinkish-white, May-blooming flowers. As the plant is neither easy to dig up nor grow, it is better to start with rooted specimens from dealers. Sand myrtle is one of our rarest wild plants and a choice, beautiful evergreen.

SANDWORT. *Arenaria caroliniana.* A chickweed-like perennial abundant on sandy wastes, but with white flowers more showy than any chickweed, and borne on almost thread-thin stalks in May. The plant is densely tufted and has many minute, pin-like leaves that are scarcely ½ inch long. Few dealers carry it, so that it must generally be dug up from the wild, which is not easy as it has a deep taproot for so small a plant. The writer has seen this growing in pure white sand that registered 130° at mid-day in July.

SEASHORE PLANTS

If not many plants will grow in pure sand, fewer still will tolerate sand impregnated with salt. That makes seashore gardening a hazard, and without costly removal of sand, replacement by better soils, and effective screening against wind, the seaside garden is not one to be undertaken lightly. Such made gardens by the sea one can find in many wealthy resorts, but this is beyond the means of most of us, and beyond the inclination of those who love the dunes, cherish the ability of a few native plants to survive the rigors of ceaseless wind, often intense heat, and a pretty heavy dose of salt.

But dunes may shift (they have inundated valuable farms in France and New Zealand), and it is often important to capture this wind-shifting sand before you can safely build even the simplest house on the dunes. Fortunately there is a remedy provided by a plant that is found on sea beach dunes practically throughout the world. Everywhere except here it is known as marram grass, but along the Atlantic and Pacific Coasts we call it simply beach grass. The scientists call it *Ammophila breviligulata* (or *Ammophila arenaria* in some books), but whatever its correct Latin name it is the one remedy for stopping the movement of sand on the dunes.

Beach grass is tough, and rough on its leathery leaf-margins. In fact by rubbing these margins the wrong way (that is, against its minute marginal teeth) you can easily slit your finger. Its great virtue is that it has a fairly deep but horizontally creeping rootstock. It is these roots that must be dug up in the fall, cut into sections of about 4 inches long, and replanted about 6 inches apart each way, and not over 3–4 inches deep.

The leaves are about 2 feet high, very wiry, and the plant tends to grow in bunches or clumps. A year or two after it is planted these clumps will be thick enough to act as a sand binder and will ultimately solve the problem of wind-blown sand. No other plant is so valuable for this purpose.

Other plants on the dunes or behind them, while of less use as sand-binders than beach grass, are far more colorful, and it is these that the sea-beach gardener will want to naturalize. If they don't happen to be on your section of the beach a short walk will soon disclose them. All of them should be dug up when dormant and planted in pure sand.

Some seaside gardeners fail to make a distinction between the plants of the dunes, which are nearly always dry, and on days of a land breeze very hot, and the plants that grow in sand behind the dunes, often on flat places, and frequently in wet ones. If wet, it is often with the brackish water of the salt marshes that are so common throughout the Atlantic coast.

It is important, however, to make this distinction, for the plants in the following brief list are not salt marsh plants at all, neither do they generally grow "with their feet in the water." There are many beautiful plants in the salt marshes, like *Sabatia,* samphire, an aster or two, sea lavender, the salt marsh mallow, and others known by those who tramp the marshes. But people do not live on the marshes, and, if these places are colorful with wild plants that withstand the salt tides, the plants are best left there and out of our garden efforts.

The plants suited to beach sand, the dunes, and the areas behind the dunes that are not wet comprise only the following. Other species grow there, but are of little use to the seaside gardener.

Beach Pea. *Lathyrus maritimus.* A sprawling or erect perennial, not over 30 inches high, usually much less, with compound leaves and striking, pea-like, blue-purple flowers, followed by a pea-like pod filled with many seeds. At the end of each leaf there may be a thread-like tendril. This is one of the showiest of all beach plants, the flowers almost rivaling the sweet pea. It blooms in midsummer and is sometimes called *Lathyrus japonicus.*

Beach Sandwort. *Honkenya peploides.* A fleshy perennial, often forming dense colonies or mats, the stems not over 12–15 inches high and clothed with thick, fleshy leaves. At the top is a sparse cluster of not very conspicuous, dirty-white flowers in June or July. If native plants were common on sea beaches, no one would trouble to grow the beach sandwort or beach purslane as some call it. Often it grows almost down to high-tide mark.

DUSTY MILLER. *Artemisia Stelleriana.* Not to be confused with the dusty miller of ordinary gardens, this densely hairy, white-velvety perennial is common in most sandy places along the seashore. It has much-divided leaves and yellow, not very showy flowers lasting from June to September. It grows rather stiffly, often up to 30 inches high, and while supposed by some to be native in Kamchatka, it certainly looks wild and, in some places, is very common from New England to Virginia.

FALSE HEATHER. *Hudsonia tomentosa.* A heath-like low perennial, often forming dense mats or patches that may be 20–30 inches across, while the individual stems are not usually over 6–8 inches high. Leaves very numerous and very small, tightly pressed against the stem, which thus seems leafless. The flowers are tiny, yellow, solitary at the end of each stalk, but *en masse* rather showy in June or July. It is one of the best ground-covering plants on the dunes, but not on their peaks or where the sand is shifting. It will also grow in interior, salt-free, sandy places, as does its close relative *Hudsonia ericoides.*

SEA ROCKET. *Cakile edentula.* An annual, rather weedy herb, 4–12 inches high, with fleshy, alternate leaves, and a few, rather inconspicuous, purplish-white flowers, mostly in midsummer. As it is an annual it can be started only from collected seed, which is reasonably plentiful by late August, and should be planted immediately for germination the following spring. Perhaps not worth growing, but it grows just above high-tide mark and will stand any amount of salt spray.

SEA-BEACH GOLDENROD. *Solidago sempervirens.* Well-named *sempervirens,* this handsomest and most sturdy of all our native goldenrods, looks as though it would live forever. It is, of course, a perennial, 18–50 inches high, with handsome, thickish leaves, without any marginal teeth. The small, yellow flower heads are in a dense, branched cluster which is perhaps more showy than any of the goldenrods of thickets or woods. It grows in pure sand, but also at the edges of salt marshes, and does not begin to bloom until early in September.

Those who have seen acres of the bearberry growing in the sandy wastes behind the dunes, and even on cindery railway embankments, may wonder why this incomparable ground-cover is not included here. The plain fact is that it is difficult to grow and is hence included in the last chapter, meant only for the expert and patient.

Swamp, Marsh, Meadow, or Bog?

CHAPTER V

MANY *WILD NATIVE* plants must have their roots in wet soil or even in open water. Some grow in the shade, others in the sun, some in sand, others in muck, some in fresh, clear water, others in "black" water. The number of different habitats that have only water as their common feature are at least four, and others could be distinguished if they mattered to the wild gardener.

What does matter is that the cultivator of wild plants ought to be able to tell the difference between the four ecological conditions signified by the words that head this chapter. In nature the differences are profound, and as we are trying to work with rather than against nature, it is well to know what she has developed and what kinds of plants are suited to each of the different environments. Definitions therefore become a necessity, before any attempt to sort out the plants which "like" wet places enough so that they grow in no other.

Swamp. A wet place characterized by trees or shrubs, hence always more or less shady. Many plants that grow naturally in such places often creep out into more open sites. All of them are of easy culture, so long as there is some shade and plenty of water in the soil, which is usually a deep loam or muck, not generally acid. Most swamps have the soil and water in them with a pH of about neutrality, that is, pH 6.5 to pH 7.5. The only exceptions are noted at the individual species if significant.

Marsh. A usually considerable tract of wet land, typically characterized by relatively tall, coarse herbs, of which the cat-tail marshes are the most familiar. Marshes are always wet, never have any trees or shrubs (unless there are mounds or hummocks) and hence no shade. Certain types of marshes cover thousands of acres in some parts of the country, notably the salt marshes along the sea coast and the canebrakes of the South. Except for these specialized types of marshes, which do not here concern us, most marsh plants are of easy culture. Some marsh plants also get into swamps and a few are sometimes found in the next category.

Meadow. A field-like tract of wet or wettish land usually dominated by grasses and wild flowers, but not by tall, coarse herbs like the cat-tail, and with no shrubs or trees. Familiar examples are the alpine meadows above the timber line on mountains, where grow some of our most beautiful wild flowers. Unfortunately the plants from alpine meadows cannot be included here, for their culture depends upon conditions rather difficult to imitate. Meadow plants are easy to grow, except where specially noted, and often creep into marshes or swamps, almost never into the next category.

Bogs. The most specialized and difficult of all wet environments, although very common in many parts of the country, familiar examples being the cranberry bogs. Sometimes there are trees in the bog, such as the spruce bogs of the north. These might hence be called a *swamp,* according to our definition of that term, were it not for a very profound difference between bogs and any other low wet place. In a true natural bog there is little or no drainage out of it, and typically it is covered by a few inches or many feet (in quaking bogs) of sphagnum moss. Much technical literature exists as to whether bogs are acid because sphagnum moss grows in them, or whether the moss grows there because bogs are naturally acid. The water in bogs is always coffee-colored, and if there are deep pools in it the water appears to be black. Generally the pH in a bog will run about pH 4–5. Few ordinary plants will survive such acidity.

Unless one or more of these wet conditions is found naturally on your property, no one is advised to create any one of them, except perhaps a bog, which is noted at that section of this chapter. Nature has developed each of them by a continuous process of evolution, at no cost to anyone, and any attempt to imitate what nature has not provided is not only very expensive, but quite likely to fail. The brief definitions above are a vast oversimplification of the many ecological details that make swamps, marshes, meadows, and bogs what they are. Consequently the lists below are simply guides as to how to utilize existing features of your site, but not to change it. Almost the only change needed in these wet places is to provide stepping stones or narrow paths, because getting about in such places is often impossible, particularly in wet weather.

SWAMP

The plants below are typically swamp plants, but many of them have a tendency to creep into marshes or meadows, although few plants from the open sites are likely to migrate into such a shady environment as a swamp. Swamps will already have the natural shade of the trees and shrubs that grow in such places, and, to make room for some of the herbs, you may have to clear out too-dominant shrubs. It is generally wise to cut out as few shrubs as possible and naturalize the perennials in small patches or even individually if the plants are tall and showy.

Most of them are of the easiest culture, so long as their roots are in a wet place and there is at least some shade. A good many of them are available from dealers in native plants, and many swamps will already have in them at least some of the plants in the list below. Many ferns, besides those mentioned in Chapter II, will also be found growing naturally. Mostly native American plants are included, as some swamps have been so much crowded with exotic material that they look like bits of European or Asiatic landscape rather than an American swamp.

Quite a few plants that grow in moist woods will also grow in swampy places. These were noted in Chapter II and the details should be sought there for the following:

Clintonia. *Clintonia borealis.*
Dog's-tooth violet. *Erythronium americanum.*
Jack-in-the-pulpit. *Arisaema triphyllum.*
Mitrewort. *Mitella diphylla.*
Snakeroot. *Cimicifuga racemosa.*
Spring beauty. *Claytonia virginica.*
Virginia cowslip. *Mertensia virginica.*

Typically swamp plants that are worth cultivating for such sites are:

ASTER. *Aster.* Most of the native asters are plants of open thickets or woods and should be sought in the chapters on those sites, but two of them grow best with their roots in wet soil. Both bloom in late summer.

New England Aster. *Aster novae-angliae.* One of the showiest of native asters, usually with clustered stems 12–35 inches high, and almost stem-clasping leaves. Flower heads red-purple, nearly 1½ inches wide, the rays very numerous. It grows in a variety of moist places and is perfectly suited to swamps that are not too densely shady. It can be easily dug from the wild, preferably when dormant. It has been the parent of many Michaelmas daisies. (See Color Plate 17.)

New York Aster. *Aster novi-belgi.* A stout perennial, 10–30 inches high, the leaves scarcely stem-clasping. Flower heads blue (sometimes whitish) about 1 inch wide, often solitary and long-stalked, or in an open, lax cluster. It grows in swamps or marshes and sometimes along the edge of salt marshes.

Cardinal-flower. *Lobelia cardinalis.* An extremely showy perennial 20–30 inches high. Flowers scarlet, irregular, extremely handsome, in a long, terminal, spire-like cluster. It inhabits swamps, but often gets into wet ditches, and blooms in midsummer. (See Color Plate 22.) Its close relative the blue lobelia, *Lobelia siphilitica,* is 20–30 inches high and has similar flowers, but blue, which are very handsome in late summer. Both the lobelias are easily moved, when dormant, and make fine wild garden material for swamps and other wet places. (See Color Plate 21.)

False Hellebore. *Veratrum viride.* A bold, striking swamp herb, its extremely poisonous root the source of a new drug for high blood pressure, known as *veratrine.* The plant is 3–5 feet high and clothed all the way up the stem with immense, plaited and deeply veined leaves. Flowers small, greenish-yellow, numerous in an open, branched cluster, blooming in June or July. A very handsome swamp plant, sometimes in early spring mistaken for the skunk-cabbage which is excluded here and should be from your wild garden on account of its evil odor.

Crested Iris. *Iris cristata.* This common, nearly stemless iris of ordinary gardens is native in the swamps of our southeastern states, and perfectly hardy in the north, up to Boston. It can thus be used along paths in the swamp garden and grows scarcely 5 inches high. Its pale lilac flowers which bloom in April are a month earlier than any of the common garden irises. For other iris species that grow in wet places, see the section on meadows in this chapter.

IRONWEED. *Vernonia noveboracensis.* A tall, stout, fall-blooming perennial, often 5–6 feet high, with narrow willow-like leaves, and a loose, open, more or less flattish flower cluster. Flower heads bluish-purple, not very showy, but attractive in late August and September. It is not quite a typical swamp plant, for it grows naturally not only in swamps, but also in meadows and even on marshes, mostly along the coast from Massachusetts to the Gulf of Mexico, and a little inland as far as Ohio.

MARSH MARIGOLD. *Caltha palustris.* In spite of its name the marsh marigold is a typical swamp plant. Like many others it often creeps out into wet ditches, meadows, and even into bogs in the far north. It has a sprawling habit, deeply heart-shaped leaves and yellow, buttercup-like flowers in mid-April or early May. Of the easiest culture and often rampant in nature. In some parts of the country it is called cowslip, although it is not related to the true cowslips. (See Color Plate 27.)

MEADOW-RUE. *Thalictrum dioicum.* A graceful, erect, often arching perennial, 12–30 inches high, the leaves compound with the ultimate divisions suggesting the maiden-hair fern. Flowers greenish-yellow, without petals, but numerous enough in the branched cluster to be showy in April or May. It is equally at home in swamps or meadows and may sometimes be found in moist woods. Carried by most dealers and easy to grow. Another species, *Thalictrum polygamum,* known as Tall Meadow-rue, is shown in the accompanying sketch.

SPIDERWORT. *Tradescantia virginiana.* A rather weak, watery-stemmed perennial, not usually over 15 inches high,

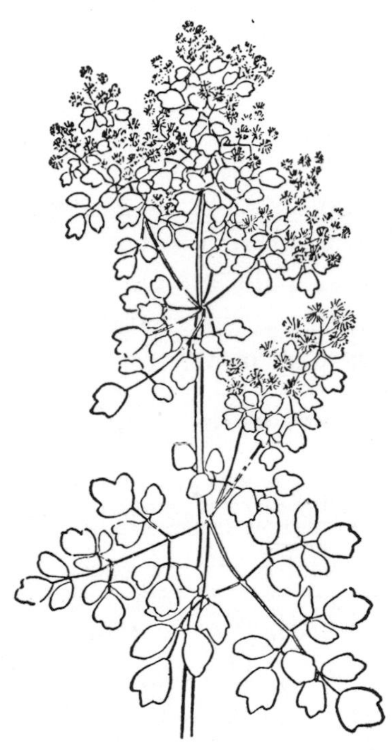

TALL MEADOW-RUE

with long narrow leaves. Flowers showy, blue or bluish-purple, very evanescent, in few-flowered clusters, the three petals nearly ¾ inch long and pointed. It is a delicate, fragile plant, easily broken at the joints, and must be handled with care, although it is not difficult to grow when once established. Summer-blooming. (See Color Plate 6.)

Swamp Milkweed. *Asclepias incarnata.* In midsummer it is a common sight to see bees and butterflies hovering over the great ball-like clusters of the pinkish-red, showy flowers of this handsome milkweed. It is a stiff erect herb, 3–5 feet high, often branched, the foliage and stems with a milky juice. It needs space and can be grown either in swamps or marshes; it is also found in wet ditches. Do not attempt to dig it out until the white, showy, fluffy seeds have been discharged from the long narrow pods. For a related milkweed see the pleurisy-root in the third chapter.

Sunflower. *Helianthus angustifolius.* A tall, rather weedy sunflower, often 3–6 feet high, its narrow leaves scarcely ½ inch wide and generally hairy. Flower heads not very numerous, about 2½ inches wide, yellow, summer-blooming. Common in swamps and even in other wet places, this sunflower is easily dug from the wild, preferably in autumn or early spring.

Sweet Flag. *Acorus calamus.* Often called calamus, the sweet flag is the commercial source of calamus root, which is aromatic, used in perfumery, and still a home remedy for colic. It is a coarse herb, with thick, sword-shaped leaves, 3–5 feet long, and a finger-shaped, close cluster of almost microscopic, yellowish-brown flowers. Easily propagated by division of its long, branching, thick rootstocks. It grows wild in dense masses and may become a nuisance in the swamp garden, unless rigorously controlled.

Turtlehead. *Chelone glabra.* This late-summer-blooming perennial is a stiff, perfectly smooth plant 18–24 inches high, growing almost exclusively in swamps and a useful plant in the swamp garden. The showy, pink or purplish flowers that are usually tinged with white, are about 1½ inches long, very irregular, and crowded in a dense terminal spike. The plant is available from most dealers and is easily grown.

WATER ARUM. *Calla palustris.* Somewhat suggesting the calla lily of the florists, but smaller, this herb of swamps often grows in the open water of pools or quiet streams. It is not over 8–10 inches high, with pointed, broadish leaves that

WHITE TURTLE-HEAD

are about 4 inches long. Above them, on a single stalk is the scarcely hooded, shallow white "flower," which may be prolonged into a short tip and is often greenish-tinged. Actually the minute flowers are crowded on the club-like spadix in the center of the white spathe. It has creeping rootstocks that root at the joints, and so it is easy to propagate, but prefers cool swamps of the north rather than those of the south.

Russell Tinling Pansie

EASTERN HAREBELL
Campanula intercedens

Harold D. Roberts

CANADIAN SHOOTING-STAR
Dodecatheon pauciflorum

C. E. Simmons, Photographer, Buffalo Museum of Science

GRASS-PINK
Limodorum tuberosum

Clyde Fisher

CARDINAL-FLOWER
Lobelia cardinalis

Cassius H. Watson

BLUE MORNING-GLORY
Pharbitis purpurea

There are, of course, many other native swamp plants, but those above will give the swamp garden a good start and bloom from mid-April until late in the fall. It should be emphasized that plants of meadows and marshes will often grow in swamps, especially if the shade is not too dense, but the general tendency is for some swamp plants also to tolerate the open sunshine of meadows and marshes. If you are in any doubt as to whether your area is swamp, meadow, or marsh, it is well to look over the plants in these sections of this chapter. Bog plants are so specialized that they are mostly confined to such places and are not generally fit for swamp, meadow, or marsh.

MARSH

To draw a distinction between marsh and meadow is not too easy, for they are both treeless, have no shrubs, plenty of water, and continuous sunshine. Actually the difference is between the types of natural vegetation that inhabit the two sites. Marsh plants are generally tall, rather coarse, and often occur in exclusive growths such as the cat-tail; meadow plants are lower, apt to be isolated or grow in open patches or mats, but scarcely ever to the exclusion of other plants.

As most people will not have a natural marsh on the place, fewer plants are in the marsh list. But many properties may run down to the edge of a marsh and hence you may find it useful to know a few plants worth naturalizing in such places. Some of them are so rampant that they may soon monopolize the area; they should be planted sparingly and watched if they tend to become a nuisance. Such precautions will be noted in the brief list below. There is no difficulty in growing any of them.

Boneset. *Eupatorium perfoliatum.* A tall, coarse, very hairy perennial, 3–8 feet high, the rough leaves in pairs through the base of which the stem passes. Flowers very small, in a large flat-topped cluster that may be 3–6 inches wide, and summer-blooming. It was called boneset from its reputed efficacy in curing "tired" bones in colonial America. Not an invasive plant and useful for bold effects in midsummer.

BURNET. *Sanguisorba canadensis.* A stiffish, spirea-like perennial, with compound leaves, the stalked leaflets toothed. Stems erect, 20–35 inches high, the tiny, white flowers crowded in a finger-shaped, rather showy cluster; summer-blooming. It grows naturally in marshes, but often invades meadows. There is no danger of it becoming a rampant pest.

CAT-TAIL. *Typha latifolia.* A dangerous plant to introduce anywhere unless you want it to capture the place, or can control its spread, which is not easy. Its long, handsome, sword-shaped leaves are 4–5 feet high and the cat-tail (actually a crowded flower cluster) may be on stalks 5–9 feet high. It has coarse creeping rootstocks, easy to chop up for propagation, but so invasive that cat-tails cover many square miles in some marshes. It has a close relative, *Typha angustifolia,* which has narrower leaves and is more common along the coast.

PICKEREL-WEED. *Pontederia cordata.* Common in muddy marshes, and even in brackish ones, the pickerel-weed is one of our most showy water plants. It thrives even after sporadic submergence. The plant is 10–30 inches high, its large, long-stalked leaves with a broad, heart-shaped blade. The plant is closely related to the water hyacinth, and has almost orchid-like, blue-violet flowers that are very showy in June and July. Pickerel-weed is apt to be invasive and needs watching if you do not want it to capture muddy shores and sometimes open water.

PURPLE LOOSESTRIFE. *Lythrum salicaria.* A showy Eurasian herb that has become so naturalized in our marshes that it looks like a native. It is a stiffish perennial 24–40 inches high, with opposite or clustered leaves, and a tall, terminal spike of reddish-purple, very handsome flowers, mostly in August-September. The plant is so desirable that it is carried by most nurserymen, who have many horticultural varieties of it. The original marsh plant is better for untamed marshes. (See Color Plate 9.)

ROSE MALLOW. *Hibiscus moscheutos.* This and a relative, the marshmallow (*Althaea officinalis*), both grow in brackish marshes, the latter, like the purple loosestrife having become so completely naturalized that few would suspect its European origin. Both are adaptable plants, for they can be planted in fresh-water marshes and even in ordinary garden soil. The rose mallow is the handsomer of the two, is erect-growing, 2–3 feet high, and in August bears white or pink, showy flowers 2–3 inches wide, some of which have a dark red spot or "eye" in the center. It grows easily from divided roots and, although it seeds freely, it is not invasive.

SNEEZEWEED. *Helenium autumnale.* A tall perennial, 3–6 feet high, its yellow flower heads 2–3 inches wide, and mostly blooming late in August. Its original home is wet marshes or other low ground, but it has long been cultivated in ordinary gardens where it thrives. It will grow well in any low, wet place, usually becoming taller in such sites. Not one of the prize swamp plants, but useful for its yellow, autumnal bloom.

WATER HEMLOCK. *Cicuta maculata.* Related to the hemlock (not a tree) used to kill Socrates. Our native plant is just as poisonous if eaten. It is a branching herb, 2–5 feet high, with compound leaves and an open, flat-topped cluster of minute, white flowers, which usually stand up above the foliage, and suggest those of Queen-Anne's lace. It grows indifferently in swamps or meadows, but is less likely to be found in marshes.

WATER HEMLOCK

MEADOW

Everyone is charmed to walk over springy meadows in May or earlier, for they are sure to be covered with sheets of wild flowers. It is these that conjure up moods so well expressed by the poets. Here one finds the delicate bluets, or Quaker ladies as many prefer to call them. It is the meadows of England dotted with squill, the primrose, and asphodel that Shakespeare and Wordsworth have immortalized.

Not many of us can have a true meadow, and practically no one will have an alpine meadow filled with gentians and saxifrage, and maybe dotted with the tiny dwarf rhododendron all of which grow above timber line on the highest mountains.

This need not keep us from growing some typical meadow plants if we have a low, grassy place free of the dominant giants of the marshes, and so favored by drainage that the place is never really dry. Nor is it ever submerged except for a few hours after a downpour. Quite often, in the north, meadows are underlaid by slabs of rock over which there may be a layer of soil only a few inches thick. In such places, if it is a real meadow, the water trickles over the rock, keeps the soil constantly moist and bathes the roots of meadow plants in cool water. This is the ideal condition, but many springy meadows have no rock and are still admirable sites for the plants in the list below.

A modification of the meadow, and perhaps not strictly entitled to be called one, is the flat, sandy place along the coastal plain that because of topography is nearly always wet. In them grow a group of wild flowers well worth cultivating. Some places, also, have meadow-like sites where there is a miscellaneous growth of herbs, none of them of any particular interest. These places often can be made to grow the more showy plants in the list below by a bit of clearing out of unwanted material.

Because they are, or should be nearly always wet, meadow gardens will need stepping stones or paths. Some New England pastures, with their scattered rocks, are practically ready for the planting of meadow species, and the rocks with a little manipulation will form natural stepping stones.

Some meadow plants, like the blue flag or the water flag, are so adaptable that, in spite of their natural habitat being in meadows, they are now widely cultivated in gardens. All the plants in the brief list below can be purchased from dealers in native plants, and this is the easiest and quickest way to get them established.

Atamasco Lily. *Zephyranthes atamasco.* A lily-like herb springing from an onion-like bulb; usually not over 15 inches high, with long, narrow leaves. The flower stalk bears a single, funnel-shaped, white flower, about 3 inches long, often tinged with purple or sometimes all purplish. It is native from Virginia southward, but is hardy up to New York. Western species, often known as fairy lily, are generally not hardy outdoors, so that our single eastern species is a prize. Ours is best started, preferably in masses, from purchased bulbs, planted about 3 inches deep in autumn.

Bluets. *Houstonia caerulea.* Called also Quaker ladies and innocence, perhaps from its tiny bonnet-like lavender-blue flowers. It is scarcely 6 inches high, with very small leaves, the flowers solitary on slender stalks, but as the plant grows in mats, very numerous. Each flower is scarcely more than ½ inch wide, with a yellow dot (eye) in the center. In some meadows it may carpet the ground with its pale blue or lavender-blue flowers, mostly in May. (See Color Plate 14.) It should only be planted in masses, as should its close relative *Houstonia serpyllifolia,* which, however, is better suited to mountain (not alpine) meadows.

Featherbells. *Stenanthium gramineum.* pH 4–5. A stout perennial taller than most meadow plants, as its erect stiffish stem may be up to 40 inches high, less as usually cultivated. It has grass-like, but keeled leaves and a tall, loose cluster of greenish-white, small flowers, usually in August or early September. Best established by purchased plants, preferably in a site that is naturally or can be made acid. In many catalogs the plant is still listed under its old but incorrect name of *Stenanthium robustum.*

Grass-of-Parnassus. *Parnassia glauca.* pH 7–8. A curious and interesting plant for meadows in limestone regions, but not recommended if your meadow soil or water is acid. It has mostly basal leaves, but on the flower stalk, which is 8–15 inches high, there is a single, stem-clasping leaf. Flowers solitary, white, waxy and suggesting an anemone, nearly one inch wide August-blooming. The plant was long known as *Parnassia caroliniana* and will usually be found under that name in the catalogs. Its culture is not at all difficult in the right kind of meadows, and the plant is relatively rare.

IRIS. *Iris.* Among the native species of iris there are two meadow kinds most worth growing:

Blue flag. *Iris versicolor.* Often called wild iris, although there are many other native species. It is a stout perennial with arching, sword-shaped leaves, not over 15–20 inches high. In May or June the handsome, almost orchid-like flowers that are prevailingly blue-violet, but blotched with yellow, are very showy. Easily increased by division of its stout rootstocks. (See Color Plate 4.)

Water flag. *Iris pseudacorus.* A European iris that has become so much at home in meadows and ditches as to appear native. It is from 20–30 inches high, has bright yellow flowers, usually in May, and is of the easiest culture.

Both these irises are carried by most nurserymen and often cultivated in ordinary garden soil; but they are typically meadow plants. For another iris of wet places, see the crested iris in the section on swamps in this chapter.

LILY. *Lilium.* For the native lilies that grow in woods, see Chapter II. There are, however, two fine, native lilies that grow in meadows (and sometimes in any wet place). Both are best started from purchased bulbs planted in autumn.

Turk's-cap Lily. *Lilium superbum.* A tall, striking lily, often reaching 5–6 feet high in the wild; usually less as cultivated. Most of its lower leaves are in clusters, but the upper ones opposite each other. Flowers very showy, nodding, the recurved petals reddish-orange, prominently purple-spotted; summer-blooming. Plant bulbs 5 inches deep. See Color Plate 27.

Wild Yellow Lily. *Lilium canadense.* A lower plant than the Turk's-cap, and not usually over 30 inches high, its leaves in clusters of 5–12. Flowers one to a few, nodding, orange-yellow or yellow, purple-spotted on the inside, the petals only slightly recurved; summer-blooming. Plant bulbs 10 inches deep.

MEADOW BEAUTY. *Rhexia virginica.* pH 4–5. A delicate, rather fragile herb, about 8–15 inches high, its 4-angled stem conspicuously hairy with scattered, stiff hairs. Leaves stalkless, opposite each other, the margins hairy. Flowers purple, nearly 1 inch in diameter, with 4 petals; August-blooming. It grows naturally in the sandy meadows and should not be attempted unless you have such a site, or can make one with sand and peat. It must be decidedly acid, and the meadow beauty often inhabits bogs, probably because they are usually acid. (See Color Plate 10 (as deergrass).)

MIST-FLOWER. *Eupatorium coelestinum.* Somewhat resembling a tall version of the garden ageratum, the mist-flower is a showy meadow plant blooming in August or September. It is 12–30 inches high, usually branched, and has many small, button-like, blue or violet-blue, misty flower-heads, borne in close clusters. Easily grown and carried by most dealers. For related plants in the genus *Eupatorium,* in swamps, dry places, or woods, see the index.

TICKSEED. *Coreopsis rosea.* pH 6. A rather weak-stemmed, but erect perennial 8–15 inches high, its leaves almost thread-like. Flower heads not very numerous, about 1 inch wide, its pink rays down-pointing, as though pulled down from the central crown; August-blooming. It grows naturally in wet, sandy meadows, or even in the water, in a mildly acid site, generally along the coastal plain. For other tickseeds, see Chapter III.

TURKEY-BEARD. *Xerophyllum asphodeloides.* pH 4–5. A stiff, stout perennial, with a single stalk 18–35 inches high springing from a mass of basal, thread-like leaves that may be as much as 12–15 inches long. Flowers about ½ inch wide, hundreds of them crowded at the top of the long stalk, mostly in June, the plant thus very showy. It grows, along the coast, mostly in wet, decidedly acid sand, but in the mountains from Virginia to Tennessee in dry woods. Best started from purchased plants.

WILD HYACINTH. *Camassia scilloides.* This is the only eastern species of a group of western plants called quamash, one of which was eaten by the Indians, and most of which are not particularly well suited to eastern gardens. Ours is a bulbous plant, 10–20 inches high with basal, narrow leaves and a terminal, loose cluster of blue or bluish-violet flowers suggesting a scilla. It blooms in April or May and is best started from purchased bulbs, planted in fall, about 3 inches deep, preferably in masses. It will also grow in ordinary garden soil if it is reasonably moist, but better if grown in wet meadows.

BOG

The successful cultivation of bog plants emphatically demands a bog. It is useless to grow them in ordinary garden soil, and most of them will not tolerate the mere wetness of a swamp, marsh, or meadow. On the contrary, few of the plants mentioned elsewhere in this book will tolerate the natural acidity that is in nearly all bogs. A few specialized bogs, in limestone regions, appear to be either alkaline, or they have acid pockets in which typical bog plants will thrive. For our purposes we can ignore such unusual sites.

How to recognize a bog, if you think you have one? Many gardeners wish they had a natural bog on the place, but few really have. The almost invariable signs are the following:

1. It must be wet, with little or no drainage *out* of it.
2. It will, or should, be generally covered with sphagnum. This ashy-gray moss, which is like a sponge for holding water, will not grow if the water is not about pH 4–5.
3. If there is no sphagnum, but you still suspect you have a bog, from the plants that grow there, test the water.
4. Bog water is nearly always coffee-colored and tests pH 4–5. If it is neutral or near it, you have a meadow or swamp, but no bog.
5. Some boggy places have no sphagnum moss and are often sandy or peaty. If you have such a place and the water and soil test pH 4–5, you can grow certain bog species. Such conditions are fairly common on the coastal plain, particularly in the pine-barrens, and probably result from the decomposition of plants.

So few places have a natural bog that the question is bound to arise, "Shall we make one?" It can be done and is probably the most justifiable of all attempts to create artificial sites. Expensive bogs have been made by building irregularly shaped concrete basins, 1–2 feet deep, and watertight, filled with the mixture outlined below. Such an artificial bog, with its piping for water, its neutralization of the lime in the concrete, and other problems of leveling, etc., are beyond the desires and often the purse of the average amateur.

This does not mean that you cannot have a bog if you have a level, flat place that is naturally wet or can be kept so inexpensively. Excavate about 18 inches of the natural soil and line the bottom with 5–6 inches of impervious clay. Tamp this down and water it, allowing it to stand with a little water in it for a few days. Make the banks shallowly sloping and line them with clay. In a week's time fill the bog three-quarters full of water and see how much leaks away by seepage or because you have not completely covered it with clay. If the lining is real clay it will be all but watertight, at any rate sufficiently so to make the bog feasible.

Assuming that there is no sphagnum moss on the place, one remedy would be to buy baled, untreated sphagnum which is listed by most dealers in horticultural supplies. It must be untreated to avoid the baking and chemicals with which some sphagnum has been treated to kill weed seeds and reduce its acidity! Such treated sphagnum is very useful in the garden but fatal for a bog, for you buy sphagnum to get acidity.

If there is no natural sphagnum and you want to avoid the expense of buying it, there is still another remedy. Make a mixture of one part ordinary garden loam, 2 parts sand, and 3 parts of acid peat thoroughly chopped up. Mix the ingredients to which may be added its own bulk of pine needles, if you have them; otherwise increase the ration of acid peat. Put the mixture in the bog and water it down, so that the surface of the fill is just above the water level.

This brings us to the important point of what sort of water you have. Unless it is pH 6 or even more acid, you should not use it in the bog. Rainwater is much better.

Allow the soaking mixture to stand a few days and test it for pH value. It quite likely will not be pH 4–5 at first, and it may never be if your water is too near neutrality (pH 7). In that case add aluminum sulfate at about the rate of 3 pounds to each 125 pounds of soil (that is, about a wheelbarrow load). You can increase or decrease the amount of aluminum sulfate, which should be raked into the mixture, in accordance with your weekly tests.

Ultimately you must get the bog to test pH 4–5, and to accomplish this and allow for proper settling of the material it is better to start the operation in the fall and postpone planting until the spring. Once the bog is established, there should not be too much trouble to keep the desired acidity, particularly if you can add some oak or hemlock chips or twigs to the mixture. If there is much sphagnum in it, acidity will take care of itself unless your water supply is alkaline.

The water supply, if you are lucky, may be a rivulet that flowed through the site of the bog and which you will, of course, utilize. The drainage *from* the bog should be as little as possible, as there is a good chance of leaching out acidity if there is too vigorous drainage. If your water supply is wholly artificial, simply put in enough water to keep the bog like a wet sponge. Never flood it enough to overflow its banks. Often rainfall will keep it about right; if not water it only to replace water lost by evaporation.

If all this sounds a bit formidable, it should not be forgotten that successful bogs have been going for years upon these principles, and in them are grown plants that will thrive nowhere else—bog orchids, for instance. Some years ago a talented amateur wrote a book, "Bog-trotting for Orchids." In it he pointed out that some of our most beautiful of all wild flowers are the orchids that grow only in bogs. They cannot be treated here, however, because other orchids grow in woods or even in sand and all of them are hence grouped in a special chapter. Of these the bog orchids will only grow under the conditions outlined above. Beyond the orchids, the number of bog plants is fairly limited. Some meadow plants are also suited to bogs. Of those already noted, which need not be described again, the following are worth trying in the bog:

Featherbells. *Stenanthium gramineum.*
Meadow beauty. *Rhexia virginica.*
Tickseed. *Coreopsis rosea.*
Turkey-beard. *Xerophyllum asphodeloides.*

The native bog plants worth cultivation are:

BLAZING-STAR. *Chamaelirium luteum.* Also called devil's bit. A wand-like perennial, 20–36 inches high, with mostly basal, ovalish leaves and a long, slender, spire-like cluster of small white flowers, usually in June. It is better to start with purchased plants, as the species is not common and likely to be exterminated.

BOG VIOLET. *Pinguicula vulgaris.* This extremely interesting insectiverous plant is also called butterwort. It is a stemless perennial with only 3–6 basal leaves that are ovalish, blunt at the tip, with the upper surface covered with a greasy or slimy coating. On this, insects are caught, held, killed, and digested by the plant. Flower stalk 2–6 inches high, crowned by a single violet flower about ¾ inch wide, provided with a violet-like spur. Carried by dealers in native plants and best suited to cool bogs in the north. Summer-flowering.

BUCKBEAN. *Menyanthes trifoliata.* A nearly stemless perennial with compound leaves with 3 leaflets and sheathing leaf-stalks. Flowering stalk 4–10 inches high, crowned with a loose cluster of white or pinkish flowers that are about ½ inch wide; in May or June. It is carried by most dealers in native plants, and while most at home in the far north, it will grow well in all but the warmest bogs.

CROW-POISON. *Amianthium muscaetoxicum.* An extremely poisonous herb if eaten, especially the bulb; often called fly-poison. A bulbous perennial, 12–30 inches high, the leaves mostly narrow and up to 16 inches long. Flowers white, in a dense, terminal, finger-shaped cluster, each individual flower not over ½ inch wide. Crow-poison has the remarkable capacity of thriving in bogs, but also in dry sandy places if the pH is 4–5. June-flowering.

MILKWORT. *Polygala lutea.* A beautiful little bog plant with usually several, branched stems, not over 12–14 inches high, the leaves mostly basal and without marginal teeth. The stems are crowned by a close, head-like cluster of small orange-yellow flowers in midsummer; quite showy. Unfortunately this milkwort is a biennial, so that seeds must be sown for the first year or two and these must be collected, as the plant is not generally carried by dealers. Once established it should maintain itself by self-sown seeds.

PITCHER-PLANT. *Sarracenia.* Remarkable insectiverous plants, the leaves pitcher-like or funnel-like, holding water and an acid which drowns and digests insects. The inside of the pitchers have downward-pointing hairs which permit an insect to crawl down but not up. Once caught in the liquid he is doomed. Of the ten species known only from the bogs of eastern North America, two can be grown in our area. They are:

Common pitcher-plant. *Sarracenia purpurea.* A stemless herb with a cluster of basal, pitcher-like, hollow leaves, generally more or less purplish-green. Flower stalk 6–15 inches high, crowned by a single, umbrella-shaped, reddish-purple flower about 2½ inches wide. Nearly always in sphagnum bogs; June-July-flowering. (See Color Plate 31.)

Trumpets. *Sarracenia flava.* The long, slender pitchers funnel-shaped, yellowish-green, very handsome and often 16–20 inches high. Flower yellow, solitary, on a stalk 20–30 inches high, in May. It is native further south than the common pitcher-plant and not quite hardy in the north. Both species are carried by all dealers in native plants.

SUNDEW. *Drosera.* Tiny, glistening insectivorous plants so plentifully furnished with sticky hairs that insects once alighting on a leaf are hopelessly caught, as the more they struggle the more they become entangled in the hairs. They are ultimately killed and digested. Sundews are typically bog plants, but are often found in wet sand if the pH is around 4–5. Several species are known, but the one most likely to succeed is *Drosera rotundifolia,* which has small, roundish leaves, about ½ inch in diameter, and a slender, often curving flower stalk, crowned with a few, small, white flowers, in midsummer. Sundews are not showy, but grown for interest. They may be collected from bogs or purchased and are not difficult to grow if you have a true bog.

SWAMP PINK. *Helonias bullata.* A somewhat bulbous perennial with many, basal, evergreen leaves that are 10–15 inches long, flat and narrow. From them springs a single, hollow flower stalk, crowned with a dense cluster of small, pink flowers in April or May, the plant quite showy. In spite of its name it grows mostly in bogs, particularly sandy ones. It is best started from purchased plants. (See Color Plate 26.)

Native Orchids

CHAPTER VI

M*OST OF US* think of orchids as rare exotics from tropical forests, so expensive that movie queens and a few other ladies of fortune are the only ones who ever wear them. There is just enough truth in this to make it plausible, but it is not the complete orchid story. The whole family contains over 7,500 species scattered all over the temperate and tropical world, but the vast majority of them are found only in the tropics and most of these are tree-perching, or epiphytes, as the scientists call them. These epiphytic orchids are not parasites, for they use the trees to which they are attached merely as a perch, never taking nourishment from the tree.

A few tropical orchids grow in the ground, but only a handful, and it is curious that this ability to grow in the ground is the chief difference between our native orchids and nearly all of the tropical ones. It may be news to some that we have any native orchids, for one hears far less of them than about the

PLATE 23

Harold D. Roberts

SKYROCKET
Gilia aggregata

Harold D. Roberts

LITTLE-ELEPHANTS
Elephantella groenlandica

Cassius H. Watson

VIRGINIA BLUEBELLS
Mertensia virginica

PLATE 24

Harold D. Roberts

TALL PAINTEDCUP
Castilleja miniata

Harold D. Roberts

SCARLET MONKEY-FLOWER
Mimulus cardinalis

Russell Tinling Pansie

LARGE-FLOWERED VERBENA
Verbena canadensis

PLATE 25

Russell Tinling Pansie

Oswego-tea
Monarda didyma

Hugo H. Schroder

Air-plant
Tillandsia fasciculata

Harold D. Roberts

Large Rydbergia
Rydbergia grandiflora

Russell Tinling Pansie

SWAMP-PINK
Helonias bullata

Harold D. Roberts

SEGO-LILY
Calochortus nuttallii

Harold D. Roberts

LAVENDERLEAF-PRIMROSE
Galpinsia lavandulaefolia

gorgeous blooms at the florist shops. Our native species are not so showy as those that grow in the Amazon Valley or in the Congo or Malaya. But some of them come close to it, and one of the most cherished accomplishments of the wild gardener is to grow these native and beautiful representatives of the fabulous orchid flora of the tropics.

Their culture, however, is never easy and you must, more than with many other wild flowers, study their environment and food preferences if you want to make them happy and bloom at the right time. All terrestrial orchids, for instance, get their food only by the cooperation of microscopic organisms found in the soil, sometimes attached to their roots, and in some cases actually living within the interior root tissue of the plant.

There are over 60 orchids native in the eastern part of North America, but of these less than 20 are worth cultivation, and some of these are so rare that they should never be dug up from the wild. If it is known that the site for any native orchid is to be destroyed by building, or road making, it is justified to dig it up before destruction overwhelms it. But the indiscriminate picking of orchids, and their digging up except by those who have a reasonable chance of making them grow, are the worst forms of nature vandalism. The chances of making them grow are dictated by rigid adherence to the directions given below.

Of the orchids included here, some grow only in bogs, others only in sandy woods, a few in meadows, and quite a few in deep, rich woods. Because environment is so important it is urged that you reread the first chapter, and then determine from Chapter V what the ecological conditions of sandy places, meadows, and, particularly, bogs are. It is, of course, most important to watch out for the pH value of all orchid soils. Most of the species seem to thrive only within rather narrow limits of acidity and alkalinity. Where no pH value is given it means that the plant grows naturally in neutral soil, or very close to it.

All the plants in the lists can be purchased from dealers in native material, and it is urged that the amateur always start with purchased plants. The hazards of digging out native orchids are so great, and failure so common, that it is a definite conservation move to get your plants from a dealer. Some deplore this advice upon the ground that the dealer will collect his plants from the wild and that there is thus no real conservation gain. But the dealer will not collect all his material, and if he does the chances are that he will be more expert than most of us. And in any case he will be propagating some orchids, and so can anyone if they are willing to take time and trouble.

BOG ORCHIDS

It is quite useless to attempt to grow bog orchids unless you not only have a bog, whether natural or made, but know how to manage it. Turn to the section on bogs in Chapter V, if you do not, before trying to grow any of those in the list below. All of them grow naturally in sphagnum, but are by no means confined to it, as some appear to do just about as well in acid, wet meadows.

The bog orchids most worth the attention of the amateur are:

ARETHUSA. *Arethusa bulbosa.* pH 4–5. Often called dragon's-mouth. A beautiful, small orchid with a single, grass-like leaf, which, however never appears until the flowers have withered. The latter are magenta-pink, but the lip is whitish-pink, marked with purple and yellow. The whole flower, which is solitary, is about 1½ inches long, borne on a stalk 4–9 inches high.

Arethusa is difficult to grow and seldom survives more than a year or two. It grows from a small bulb, which is not well anchored in the sphagnum. Little is really known as to its requirements, and the only safe way to move it is to put a stake alongside the blooming plant, and to dig it out only when the ground is frozen. Plunge the frozen orchid-sod in your bog and hope for the best. It is one of the flowers that should never be picked, however, as it is becoming rare.

FRINGED ORCHIDS. *Habenaria.* The showiest of all native orchids, and often called fringed orchis. Some species grow in woodlands, but these are not so showy as the bog species below. All of them are next to impossible to grow permanently, as they tend to die out after a year or two. The only hope of growing them successfully is to dig out frozen, marked clumps, plunged in your bog. No one appears to have conquered the secret of propagation from seed, which is extremely minute, and uniformly fails to germinate under artificial conditions.

The finest of the fringed orchids that are at home in bogs are:

Purple fringed orchid. *Habenaria psycodes.* pH 5–6. Stems 12–30 inches high, crowned with a terminal cluster of much-fringed, very showy, purple flowers. Grows also in wet meadows and even in open, wet woods. Perhaps our most handsome, native wild flower. Summer-blooming.

White fringed orchid. *Habenaria blephariglottis.* pH 4–5. Not quite so tall as the purple fringed orchid, usually from 10–20 inches high. The flower cluster is rather compact, almost cylindric, and about 4 inches long. The pure white, fringed flowers, which bloom in midsummer are about ¾ inch long.

Yellow fringed orchid. *Habenaria ciliaris*. pH 5–6. Stem 5–25 inches high, crowned at the top with an orange-yellow

WHITE FRINGED ORCHID

flower cluster that may be 3–5 inches long. The fringed, orange-yellow flowers are about ¾ inch long. While it is usually found in sphagnum bogs, it also grows in wet sandy, acid places.

Grass Pink. *Calopogon pulchellus*. pH 4–5. A showy and beautiful orchid, mostly 18–20 inches high, with a single, basal, grasslike leaf. Flowers only 3–12, in a terminal rather loose cluster, the individual flowers about ¾ inch long, rose-purple, but fringed with whitish, magenta- or yellow-tipped hairs. A difficult orchid to grow and only to be attempted by digging out frozen, marked clumps to be plunged in the bog. (See Color Plate 19 (as *Limodorum*).)

SNAKE-MOUTH. *Pogonia ophioglossoides*. pH 4–5. A typical bog orchid, somewhat resembling arethusa, but the single, narrow leaf always present at flowering time. The solitary flower is rose-pink or pinkish-white, and not over one inch long, its lip veined with red, and with a few yellow hairs. June-blooming. It is most difficult to grow and only likely to succeed by lifting frozen, marked clumps.

All the bog orchids that should be dug as frozen clumps will, of course, have died down to the ground long before frost. In other words, you must mark the clumps when in full flower with a stout stake. Moving them while in flower is practically certain to be a failure, and picking most of them is nothing but vandalism, since many are destroyed by merely picking the flowers. Generally it is far better to start all the bog orchids from purchased plants.

WOODLAND AND MEADOW ORCHIDS

Fortunately some of the woodland and meadow orchids are far easier to grow than any of the bog species. But one or two are so difficult that they should be attempted only by the expert or at least by those who have unlimited patience and are willing to follow the trail of those who have succeeded. Some, like the calypso, should perhaps never be attempted. Others, like the yellow lady's-slipper, go on blooming, and even spread for years—only, of course, if you have given it the right conditions.

The woodland kinds need a bit of explanation. Those

marked "rich woods" need the kind of deep, rich humus described in Chapter I. Others marked "dry, open woods" grow where the forest canopy is open, there is much filtered sunlight, and the soil is apt to be quite acid. It is, of course, important to watch for the different pH requirements. Where no pH value is stated it is understood that the plant grows naturally in a neutral or near-neutral soil.

Calypso. *Calypso bulbosa.* pH 5–6. Not over 8 inches high and usually less. A delicate, rare orchid, with one old leaf at the time of bloom, leafless all the summer, but producing its single basal leaf in autumn which persists until the plant blooms in May or June. Flower solitary, very showy, although only ¾ inch long. It is generally purplish, variously marked with white, yellow, red-brown, and with three rows of yellow hairs. Found in deep, rich, coniferous woods, mostly in the north, it almost defies cultivation and should never be attempted unless dug up while frozen and put in rich, forest humus only in the north, or at elevations of 2000–3000 feet elsewhere.

Crane-fly Orchid. *Tipularia discolor.* A summer-blooming, rare orchid, with a single basal, broadish leaf that appears only in the autumn and is gone before the flowering stalk is blooming during the following July or August. Flowers not very numerous in a loose cluster which is not over 8–15 inches high. The individual flowers are greenish-purple, and otherwise marked with pale purple and streaked with deep purple. Found in rich woods.

Five-leaves. *Isotria verticillata.* pH 4–5. Often called whorled pogonia, because of its old scientific but incorrect name of *Pogonia verticillata,* by which it is still listed in some catalogs. A curious orchid with a single cluster of five leaves near the top of the stem, above which, in May or June, is produced a single bloom. The flower consists of three long, narrow segments which are greenish-brown or purplish-brown, the rest of the much shorter segments purple and yellow. In dry, open, sandy woods and best moved when thoroughly frozen, as it is difficult to get established.

CRANE-FLY ORCHID

LADY'S-SLIPPER. *Cypripedium.* These, the most showy of our upland native orchids, contain two species that well contrast the delights and difficulties of native orchid culture. The common pink lady's-slipper or moccasin flower is extremely difficult to grow, while its yellow relative is so easy that, if one were asked to recommend only one orchid to cultivate, it would be the yellow lady's-slipper. Of the five native species the following four are available:

Moccasin flower. *Cypripedium acaule.* pH 4–5. Often called pink lady's-slipper, and a very difficult orchid to grow. It has extremely brittle but wiry, wide-spreading roots that creep just beneath the shallow, acid duff under open pine woods. It is next to impossible to dig these out without injuring them, which means certain failure. The best chance of success is to dig out a frozen clump, being careful even in midwinter to get *all the roots.* These may spread in all directions from the crown of the plant, often as much as 18 inches from it, so that at least a square yard of frozen soil must be taken and care should be used not to break the clump.

As nearly everyone knows the pink lady's-slipper has two largish, basal leaves, from which spring the flowering stalk, 8–15 inches high, crowned by the beautiful, pink, May-blooming, pouch-like or moccasin-like flower. It grows in sandy pine woods, often on acid sand, and sometimes even in moist places.

Ram's-head lady's-slipper. *Cypripedium arietinum.* pH 5. Not over 12–15 inches, the stem leafy. Leaves often folded, 2–4 inches long. Flower solitary, scarcely more than one inch long, generally greenish-brown, but partly white and streaked with red. It blooms mostly in late May or early June and grows usually in deep, rich, coniferous forests in the north. Purchased plants make the best method of starting it.

Showy lady's-slipper. *Cypripedium reginae.* The tallest and showiest of our native lady's-slippers, often reaching a height 20–30 inches, its stem leafy, with deeply veined, half-clasping, hairy leaves. Flowers usually one, sometimes two or three, very handsome, the sepals white, but the pouch whitish-pink, but streaked and spotted with purple. June-blooming. It grows in rich, moist woods, but also in swamps and even in bogs. It is best to start with purchased plants. (See Color Plate 32 (as *C. hirsutum*).)

Yellow lady's-slipper. *Cypripedium calceolus.* There are two forms of this easiest of all lady's-slippers to grow: a small-flowered and large-flowered. In many catalogs you will find the small-flowered sort listed as *Cypripedium parviflorum* and the large-flowered one as *Cypripedium pubescens.* By whatever name, they are leafy-stemmed orchids with one or two very handsome, yellow, pouch-like flowers, often veined with purple, and about 2½ inches wide. In not too dry woods and sometimes in bogs. Given these conditions it thrives readily, will flower in May or June, persist for years and spread. It is best to begin with purchased plants.

LADIES'-TRESSES. *Spiranthes cernua.* Scarcely over 5–15 inches high the stem twisted, especially that part of it that bears the flowers, which thus appear as if borne on a spirally twisted stalk. Flowers very small, white, scarcely ½ inch long, but quite numerous so that the twisted spike, if not conspicuous, is an arresting sight in midsummer. It is mostly found in grassy meadows and of easy culture. Not handled by dealers but easily dug from the wild, preferably in late fall (from marked plants).

PUTTY-ROOT. *Aplectrum hyemale.* Sometimes called Adam and Eve and resembling somewhat the crane-fly orchid, already noted, but it does not have the small spur to its flower which is characteristic of the crane-fly orchid. The putty-root bears a single evergreen leaf during winter, but this is gone by May when the flower stalk appears, which may be 12–18 inches high. Flowers purplish-brown, but the white lip violet-streaked. Grows in rich woods, but is difficult to establish. It is so rare that picking its flowers is inexcusable.

PUTTY-ROOT ORCHID

RATTLESNAKE PLANTAIN. *Goodyera pubescens.* pH 5–6. Often listed in catalogs under the incorrect names of *Epipactis* or *Peramium.* This little plant with basal, white-marked leaves is our only orchid with variegated leaves. It is not a showy plant, having a terminal spike of small, greenish-white flowers in midsummer. The flowering stalk scarcely more than 8–12 inches high. Grows mostly in dry, moderately open woods, but, as it is handled by most dealers, purchased plants are best to start with.

Showy Orchis. *Orchis spectabilis.* pH 5–6. A stout and almost spectacular orchid, 6–15 inches high, with apparently only two basal leaves that are bright green, 5–9 inches long. The spike is few-flowered, but each May-blooming flower is about one inch long and purplish-pink, but the lip is pure white, the effect being most striking. In rich woods and if dug when dormant and given the proper conditions, not difficult to grow. It apparently prefers somewhat moist woods. (See Color Plate 32 (as *Galeorchis*).)

Tway-blade. *Liparis liliifolia.* An interesting orchid of fairly rich woods, not over 8 inches high, with two basal leaves and a loose cluster of not very conspicuous flowers which are generally purplish-green, but not over ½ inch long. It grows from a solid bulb and is best started from purchased plants. It blooms from late June to early July.

Only for the Expert or Patient Grower

CHAPTER VII

ONLY *THE EXPERT* and the patient amateur wild gardener will be painstaking enough to conquer the hazards of growing the few but admittedly difficult native plants in the list that follows. All but one of them belongs to the heath family or what the botanists call Ericaceae. To that family also belong azalea, rhododendron, the mountain laurel, and many other shrubs and trees. All plants in the heath family, like the orchids treated in Chapter VI, have devious and often unexplained methods of getting their food from the highly specialized soil-environment in which they grow.

Basically, without wandering off in a maze of technicalities, these plants of the heath family have at or within their roots many microscopic organisms (mostly fungi but often bacteria) upon which they depend for their food supply. There is no doubt that this association of living root hairs of the plant and the microscopic organism attached to or even within them is of mutual benefit. This association is roughly called by the experts a form of *symbiosis* (literally living together). To this form of symbiosis has been attached the term *mycorrhizal* symbiosis (*myco* is Greek for "fungus" and *rhiza* for "root"). In other words mycorrhizal plants, like nearly all the heath family, the oaks, beeches, and many other plants, do not have simple and direct methods of getting their food. Unlike a daisy or dahlia, which stands upon its own roots and leads an independent life, plants of the heath family are mycorrhizal and hence not autophytes—that is, they do not rely wholly upon their own roots for their food supply. There is always some close, and often elusive, association between the root hair and a minute fungus. If the process went far enough it would, or at least it is postulated that it would, lead to outright parasitism, as it has in the Indian-pipe, which for this reason can never be cultivated.

The complex biological association of root hair and fungus lies far outside the scope of this book and is mentioned only because it has an intensely practical application in the cultivation of all the plants in this chapter except the last one. Transplanting wholly autophytic plants (that is, living unaided on their own roots) is, as we have seen, not too difficult if ordinary care is used as to soil, shade, and water. It is quite otherwise with the mycorrhizal plants of the heath family. It is not merely digging up all the roots at the right time; it is the all but impossible task of not disturbing the delicate balance between root hair and fungus. It is this task that makes dismal failure of so many misguided attempts to dig out trailing arbutus or the bearberry. No amount of enthusiasm for wild gardening, or desire to bring in some treasure of the heath family, not even the "green thumb" itself can overcome ignorance of this fundamental fact in the life history of the heath family.

Fortunately there are two methods of scaling this apparent impasse, but it is better to understand the nature of the barrier before adopting either remedy for it. Plants of the heath family, like all others in the temperate zone, have a period of semi- or total-dormancy, coinciding with winter. When the ground is frozen, roots and their attendant organisms are so nearly dormant that we can assume practically complete inactivity, especially if the ground is frozen for at least 8–10 inches, below the surface. For many shallow-rooted plants, like trailing arbutus and the bearberry, a frost depth of 3–6 inches is enough.

It is not easy to cut with a pick or old axe a frozen sod containing your plant, but it is far safer than digging it up at any other time. Plunge the frozen sod in a soil mixture to be noted presently. Actually all that is done is to "plant" your frozen sod, just as you would any other plant in the spring. Your bed must, of course, have been prevented from freezing by a deep mulch of leaves that can easily be raked off when you are ready to "plant" your sod.

The other, much more easy, but more expensive method of getting these desirable plants established is to purchase them. Various dealers and specialists in wild flowers have developed techniques whereby you can purchase potted plants of all except the last plant in this chapter. They will come with roots already developed, impregnated with the needed organism. Ordinarily they will have been propagated from seed or from cuttings, and this is the simplest and most direct way of getting them started.

Neither these pampered potted plants from the dealer nor your frozen sods from the wild will prosper unless the soil you put them in and its acidity are as near perfect as you can get them. Notes on soil mixtures are added to those that need special ones, but the acidity must be controlled by the methods already outlined in Chapter I. If watering is necessary see that your tap water is of the right pH or else use rainwater. Once established, your plants should be cared for by normal rainfall. If you have planted frozen sods they should need no water at first, since thawing in spring will release considerable moisture. Until thoroughly established, however, they should not be allowed to dry out.

The plants worth all this trouble are:

ALPINE AZALEA. *Loiseleuria procumbens.* pH 4–5. A dwarf, bushy shrub, not over 4 inches high, with tiny, evergreen, heath-like leaves crowded into dense clusters. The tiny pink or white flowers, which are scarcely ¼ inch long, are crowded in relatively dense, terminal clusters; blooming in July. The alpine azalea is fit only for cool northern regions and should be grown in a mixture of half acid peat and half sphagnum, preferably moist.

BEARBERRY. *Arctostaphylos uva-ursi.* pH 4–5. The finest evergreen groundcover in our native flora, turning bronzy in the winter. It is a long-trailing, prostrate, woody vine, with small, shiny, green leaves, tiny white or pinkish-white flowers followed by a brilliant red berry about the size of a pea. It is one of the most difficult of all wild flowers to transfer from the wild. All plants dug up during the growing season are sure to perish. If you are preparing a bed for it on anything like such a scale as its superb groundcovering quality deserves, it should be done as follows. Dig out all existing soil for a depth of 18 inches, and place in the hole a layer of coal ashes 4–5 inches deep. Upon this layer of ashes, fill in the bed with a mixture of pure sand and chopped peat moss at the rate of 5 parts of sand to 2 of peat moss. Let it settle and, after a few rains, test it for pH. Add enough aluminum sulfate to get it to pH 4–5. It is then ready for your frozen sods for winter planting or for your potted specimens from the dealer, which are best put out in early spring.

The bearberry in its native heath often grows in pure sand and along the cindery wastes of the railway on eastern Long Island and Cape Cod. But do not be misled by its apparent in-

SPOTTED WINTERGREEN

difference to tough sites. It is still one of the most difficult and desirable of all native plants to get established in cultivation.

Chimaphila. Two delightful little plants of the heath family, with evergreen leaves and small white or pink flowers, both summer-blooming. Both of them grow in dry, sandy, open woods and will do well in a mixture of one half sand and one half acid peat. Best started from purchased plants, for digging them out is hazardous. There are two kinds:

Pipsissewa. *Chimaphila umbellata*. pH 4–5. Often called prince's-pine, the whole plant 3–8 inches high. Leaves clustered, evergreen, about 2 inches long. Flowers pinkish

PLATE 27

Russell Tinling Pansie

Turkscap Lily
Lilium superbum

C. E. Simmons, Photographer Buffalo Museum of Science

Common Marsh-marigold
Caltha palustris

PLATE 28

Harold D. Roberts

LARGE-FLOWERED TROUTLILY
Erythronium grandiflorum

Hugo H. Schroder

WATER-HYACINTH
Eichhornia crassipes

Joseph R. Swain

NODDING WAKEROBIN
Trillium cernum

about ½ inch wide, in a sparse loose cluster. A useful plant in open, sandy woods.

Spotted wintergreen. *Chimaphila maculata.* pH 5–6. Resembling pipsissewa, but lower and with pointed white-variegated leaves and waxy, white flowers nearly ¾ inch wide. Fine on sandy land under oaks or pines. It does not want deep shade.

Gaultheria. Two low, creeping plants of diverse habit and also of cultural requirements. The wintergreen should be grown in open woods, preferably rather sandy, and is difficult to get established. The creeping snowberry, on the other hand, grows in sphagnum bogs and wet, coniferous woods, only in the north. The two species are:

Creeping snowberry. *Gaultheria hispidula.* pH 4–5. Often listed in old catalogs as *Chiogenes,* this tiny inhabitant of cool mountain bogs is a weak, prostrate vine with evergreen leaves 1/3 inch long, but very numerous. It has tiny white flowers in May or June, which are scarcely ¼ inch long, and nodding, followed by a small, white berry. To be grown in the bog garden and only in cool, high places.

Wintergreen. *Gaultheria procumbens.* pH 4–5. An evergreen, prostrate plant, nearly vine-like, its juice the only source of wintergreen until supplanted by the synthetic substitute. Leaves oblong, 1–2 inches long, mostly in clusters at the ends of the lax branches. Flowers barrel-shaped, about 1/3 inch long, followed by a bright red berry. It grows naturally in open, often sandy woods along the coastal plain, but also on rocky ledges in the interior. One of our most difficult plants to get established and best done from purchased plants. Put in a mixture of half sand and half chopped acid peat, thoroughly mixed.

MOUNTAIN CRANBERRY. *Vaccinium vitis-idaea.* pH 4–5. This is often called cowberry, and is a prostrate or laxly branched woody plant, never over 8 inches high, usually considerably less. It has many, small, leathery, evergreen leaves, and very few small, bell-shaped, pink or red flowers in tiny clusters, followed by a red, edible berry, nearly ½ inch in diameter. It is a delightful, prostrate evergreen groundcover, but suited only to cool bogs in the north. Purchased plants are the best method of starting it.

TRAILING ARBUTUS

TRAILING ARBUTUS. *Epigaea repens.* pH 4–5. Often called Mayflower and perhaps the most fragrant and one of the most difficult of all native plants to become established. It has evergreen, ovalish leaves, 2–4 inches long, its blades and the leaf stalk densely and softly hairy. Flowers pinkish-white, appearing in April or May, very fragrant, followed by a dry capsule containing the almost microscopic seeds. These, if not gathered immediately, are soon eaten by insects, but even if gathered are a problem to germinate. Unless you can plant them within a month or two, they must be kept at 40–50° until next spring. Plant seeds by sprinkling them on a mixture of ground-up peat moss, ground sphagnum moss, and clean sand in equal parts. Sprinkle a very little of this mixture over the seeds and water gently. The pots or pans must never be allowed to dry out and hence need constant attention. Preferably the top of the pot should be covered by a sheet of glass —all kept in the shade.

Germination should occur in 5–6 weeks, and when the seedlings are about 3 months old they may be transferred to small flower pots filled with the same soil mixture. Plunge the pots in a crate or box of sphagnum moss, and never let them dry out. Cover the pots with glass and keep them growing in the greenhouse, or hotbed, all winter. These can all be put outdoors in the spring, but kept in the same pots until the second year. They are then transferred to larger (4–5 inch) pots in which they will be carried until ready for regular outdoor planting the third spring. (See Color Plate 14.)

If all this sounds pretty difficult it explains why potted, rooted plants of trailing arbutus are rather expensive. But from them and from similar rooted plants derived from cuttings is your best hope of getting this prized treasure established in your wild garden. Prepare the place for it by digging out all soil and filling with a mixture of half sand and half chopped peat, allowed to settle, and tested until pH is 4–5. If it is not as acid as this, see the directions in Chapter I for making it so.

It is completely useless to attempt to dig up clumps of trailing arbutus from the wild, and in some states it is prohibited by law. Even picking a few flowers is to be deplored, for indiscriminate picking already threatens extermination.

GENTIAN. *Gentiana.* Very beautiful wild flowers, some of them having the purest blue flowers found in our native flora. Of the many kinds found in North America only two can be considered here, one easy and the other quite difficult. These two are:

Closed gentian. *Gentiana andrewsi.* A perennial of fairly easy culture if grown in wet places, either in partial shade or in the open. It is a stout plant, 12–18 inches high, with stiff, opposite or clustered leaves, and several deep blue flowers in a terminal, stalkless cluster in August or September. The individual flowers are like a closed bottle, never open, and the plant is often called the bottle gentian. There is no difficulty about growing it, and purchased plants are easily available.

Fringed gentian. *Gentiana crinita.* The most beautiful of all our gentians, but, alas, a biennial. These are hard enough to keep going in any ordinary garden, but far more so in the case of the fringed gentian. It is a usually unbranched plant with opposite leaves; not over 12–15 inches high. Flower stalks few, but each crowned with a solitary, beautifully fringed, blue flower nearly 2 inches high; autumn-blooming.

As seeds are seldom offered by the dealers you will have to collect your own, probably around October first. Do not keep the seed for a few weeks or months, as it will lose its germinating power. Plant at once in a mixture of one half pure sand, one half chopped peat moss, fine enough to sieve through a ¼ inch mesh of wire screening. Thoroughly mix the sand and peat and fill the pots or pans you will use,

Harold D. Roberts

PRAIRIE CONEFLOWER
Lepachys columnaris

Harold D. Roberts

RAMALEY BEEBALM
Monarda ramaleyi

William A. Pluemer

GOLDEN-CLUB
Orontium aquaticum

Wild Flower Preservation Society

WESTERN SKUNK-CABBAGE
Lysichiton americanum

leaving broken crocks or pebbles in the bottom for drainage.

Sift some of the same mixture through a finer sieve, and put about ¼ inch of this over the pot. It is in this very fine layer that you will sow the almost infinitesmal seeds. Do not cover them with the fine soil mixture, but merely press them into the soil over which you have scattered them. The pots and their contents must be kept constantly moist, preferably by plunging them in sphagnum, watered when necessary.

When the seed is planted, tie over each pot a tightly stretched piece of burlap and keep it there until the seeds germinate, which should be the following spring. The burlap is to keep heavy rains from washing out the seeds and will be removed when the seedlings, which are very small, start to grow. These burlap-covered pots will be in a lath-covered cold frame all of their first winter, and the pots, without the burlap, will be in the frame all of the following growing season.

During their first summer the seedlings should need little attention beyond watering, but the lath screen should be kept in place, and on it, when the second winter comes, it is a good plan to use a light mulch of salt hay or straw.

The second spring for the seedlings is the most critical. They must be thinned out to prevent crowding, but few of them live if transplanted. Left in their pots they will surely flower by September or October, but to lift the seedlings out as you would with ordinary ones is fatal. Perhaps the only safe way is to plunge the pot in the natural meadow which is their only rightful home, break it into pieces without disturbing the soil, and hope that the fringed gentian will not only flower and set seed, but maybe scatter some for the future. There is practically no other way of establishing the fringed gentian, and to pick the flowers of wild plants is pure murder, for only from the flower and its subsequent seed can this biennial beauty hope to survive. (See Color Plate 18.)

Native Plant Dealers

MOST REGULAR nurserymen do not carry native plants, and the wild gardener will hence find the following list of dealers most useful. The list is mostly from the files of the Massachusetts Horticultural Society, but does not cover Pacific Coast dealers as much of their material is unsuited to the East. The inclusion of any nursery does not imply approval, nor does the omission of one denote disapproval. It is always better to send for catalogs before ordering.

Will Curtis
Garden in the woods
South Sudbury, Mass.

Langley Williams
Exeter, N.H.

Putney Nursery Co.
Putney, Vt.

Red Cedar Wildflower
Nursery
U.S. Route #7
Falls Village, Conn.

Ferndale Nurseries
Askov, Minn.

Wake Robin Farm
Route #1, Box 33
Home, Pa.

Vicks Wild Gardens
Narbeth, Pa.

Exeter Wild Flower Garden
Exeter, N.H.

Virginia L. Stephenson
P.O. Box #926
Colorado Springs, Colo.

Oscar H. Will Seed Company
Bismarck, N.D.

Valley Gardens
21301 Telegraph Road
Detroit, Mich.

Claude A. Barr
Smithwick, S.D.

Pearce Seed Co.
Moorestown, N.J.

Wm. Crosby Horsford
Charlotte, Vt.

Gardenside Nurseries
Shelburne, Vt.

Green Bush Gardens
Charlotte, Vt.

Milo Kibbe
Eureka Springs, Ark.

Gardens of the Blue Ridge
E. C. Robbins
Ashford, N.C.

Curtis Nurseries
Callicoon, N.Y.

Knickelbein's Wild Life Nurseries
Jackson Drive Road
R 5, Box 26
Oshkosh, Wis.

Nik Nar
Biltmore Station
Asheville, N.C.

Lounsberry Gardens
Oakford, Ill.

Pioneer Seed Company
Dimondale, Mich.

Johnson's Nurseries
Dept. 9
Southwick, Mass.

Bay State Nurseries
North Abington, Mass.

Pavek Nursery
White Lake, Wis.

Bibliography

Aiken, George D. *Pioneering with wild flowers;* revised edition. 131 pages. Stephen Daye Press, 1946. N.Y.

Birdseye, Clarence. *Growing woodland plants,* by Clarence and Eleanor Birdseye. 223 pages. Oxford University Press, 1952. N.Y.

Durand, Herbert. *My wild flower garden.* 242 pages. G. P. Putnam's Sons, 1927. N.Y.

Durand, Herbert. *Taming the wildings.* 380 pages. G. P. Putnam's Sons, 1923. N.Y.

Hull, Helen S. *Wild flowers for your garden.* 280 pages. Barrows, 1952. N.Y.

McKenny, Margaret. *The wild garden.* 123 pages. Doubleday, 1936. N.Y.

Pellett, Frank C. *Flowers of the wild, their culture and requirements.* 160 pages. De La Mare, 1931. N.Y.

Pellett, Frank C. *Success with wild flowers.* 193 pages. De La Mare, 1948. N.Y.

Steffek, Edwin F. *Wild flowers and how to grow them.* 192 pages. Crown Publishers, 1954. N.Y.

Taylor, Norman. *Taylor's Encyclopedia of Gardening.* 1225 pages. Houghton Mifflin Co., 1948. Boston.

Index

PLATE 31

Harold D. Roberts

WESTERN BLUE FLAG
Iris missouriensis

Walter Henricks Hodge

COMMON PITCHERPLANT
Sarracenia purpurea

Wild Flower Preservation Society

HOODED PITCHERPLANT
Sarracenia minor

Lawrence D. Hiett

SHOWY LADYSLIPPER
Cypripedium hirsutum

Clyde Fisher

SHOWY ORCHIS
Galeorchis spectabilis